The Doctrine of Baptism

THOMAS PATIENT

THE
DOCTRINE
OF
BAPTISM

Edited by
Andre A. Gazal

The Doctrine of Baptism
Copyright © 2022 Andre A. Gazal
H&E Publishing, Peterborough, Ontario
www.hesedandemet.com

Source in Public Domain: Thomas Patient, *The Doctrine of Baptism, and the Distinction of the Covenants, Or A Plain Treatise, Wherein the Four Essentials of Baptism* (London: Henry Hills, 1654).

All rights reserved. This book may not be reproduced, in whole or in part, without written permission from the publishers.

Manager of reprints: Christopher Ellis Osterbrock
Cover design by Corey M.K. Hughes
Interior font: Equity Text A

Paperback ISBN: 978-1-77484-026-9
Ebook ISBN: 978-1-77484-027-6

Contents

Introduction *Andre A. Gazal*	1
Dedication	13
1. Acts 2:37–38 Laid Open	25
2. The Ordinance of Baptism Explained	29
3. Faith and Repentance Go Before Baptism	39
4. The Ordinance of Baptism Long Neglected	45
5. Two Covenants	51
6. Circumcision Proved to Be No Covenant of Eternal Life	63
7. United by Christ in Faith	103
8. Answers to Such Scriptures	109
9. Baptism & Lord's Supper	159
10. Conclusion: The Commands of Christ	167
Scripture Index	169

Introduction

In the aftermath of the English Civil War, Oliver Cromwell (1599-1658) promoted a policy of limited religious toleration during the period of his Protectorate. Even though this policy still outlawed Roman Catholicism, and greatly proscribed the practices of the Church of England as contained in the *Book of Common Prayer*, it conversely encouraged the proliferation of sects previously outlawed in England such as the Levellers, Ranters, and Fifth Monarchists as well as the Quakers and Seekers.[1]

Baptists also benefitted immensely from the Civil War and the ensuing Protectorate of Cromwell. Many Baptists served in the New Model Army as well as various areas of the government.[2] Moreover, during the years 1648-1660, Baptists experienced numerical growth.[3] Furthermore, the religious freedom afforded Baptists under the Protectorate enabled them to preach publicly, form new churches, organize associations, and openly circulate their views through printed tracts and treatises. These conditions also made it possible for Baptists to carry on their work throughout other areas of the British Isles, including Ireland.

At the forefront of Baptist activity in Ireland was Thomas Patient. A former Anglican and Independent who experienced intolerance in Puritan Massachusetts, Patient worked with William Kiffin (1616-1701) to establish and strengthen the Baptist community in Dublin as well as in many other Irish towns and cities. Significantly, Patient participated in the drafting of the

---

[1] Bill J. Leonard, *Baptist Ways: A History* (Valley Forge, PA: Judson Press, 2003), 31.

[2] H. Leon McBeth, *The Baptist Heritage: Four Centuries of Baptist Witness* (Nashville, TN: Broadman, 1987), 111.

[3] McBeth, *Baptist Heritage*, 111.

First London Confession (1644) and penned one of the most formidable Reformed critiques of infant baptism, *The Doctrine of Baptism and the Distinction of the Covenants* (1654). What follows is a brief sketch of Patient's life followed by an overview of the main argument of this important treatise.

Thomas Patient's life and career

Thomas Patient was born in Barnstable, Devonshire in 1591. Young Thomas was raised in the established Church as defined by the Elizabethan Settlement.[4] With the patronage of his uncle, Patient attended the prestigious Winchester College. Though raised in the Church of England, Patient seemed to have adopted Independent ideas relatively early as well as the platform of the Roundheads. Patient describes the process whereby he converted from the Church of England to Independency in the *Epistle to the Christian Reader* prefacing his later *Doctrine of Baptism*:

> But presently being convinced of the unwarantbleness of the Government of the Lordly Prelates, and the Liturgy in the Church of England, and the mixed communions in the parish assemblies, I was resolved, God willing, to examine all religion, as well in worship, and the order of God's house, as I had done in other points. But I at this time being by the divine power of God, converted from the Church of England, though with a great deal of difficulty, being well furnished with arguments from pulpit and print, and divers disputations for the defense of that false way; but God breaking in by the power of his Spirit with clear Scripture-light subjected my heart to the obedience of the truth, so that I found my heart closing with those truths in the love thereof.[5]

---

[4] For a more extensive discussion, see Andre Gazal, *Believers' Baptism in Cromwellian Ireland: Thomas Patient's Doctrine of Baptism* (Louisville, KY: Andrew Fuller Center for Baptist Studies, 2019).

[5] Thomas Patient, *Doctrine of Baptism*, A6.

THE DOCTRINE OF BAPTISM

Moreover, around 1616 Patient spent time at Southampton at the home of John Major, lord of the manor at Hursley, who was also an Independent and a Member of Parliament as well as the father-in-law of Oliver Cromwell's son, Richard (1626–1712).

Throughout the 1620s, Patient resided in London where he participated in the formation of the Massachusetts Bay Company. In March 1630, as a stockholder in the Company, Patient embarked with other Independents under the leadership of Governor John Winthrop (1587–1649) aboard the *Arabella* for New England. Per Patient's own testimony in his Preface to the *Christian Reader*, he left for New England as one who fully subscribed to the ecclesiastical order and practice of the Independents and the commonwealth they intended to establish in New England:

> At this time many godly Christians going to New England, and being come up in my judgment to the way of New England in faith and order, went over thither, being not convinced of my error and great darkness is sprinkling the carnal seed of believers. But verily I thought I had good warrant for that practice, having than in substance the same grounds for the defense thereof, that generally to this day is urged for the same.[6]

By Patient's own admission, he was thoroughly convinced of the validity of infant baptism at the time of his departure on the *Arabella*.

While in Massachusetts, Patient for quite some time assented to the doctrine and practice of Massachusetts' ecclesiastical commonwealth. However, he eventually began to entertain doubts about infant baptism, fearing the danger of receiving doctrine merely by tradition. Therefore, Patient proceeded to examine the biblical foundation of this doctrine. Meanwhile he

---

[6] Patient, *Doctrine of Baptism*, A6–7.

continued to attend public worship at the meeting house, endeavoring to resolve his doubts. The question of baptism proved so perplexing for Patient that he refrained from Communion until he settled it. Thus, determined to discover the truth, Patient listened to the sermons of Massachusetts' ministers on the baptism of children of believing parents. Upon analyzing the Scriptural arguments advanced in these sermons, Patient concluded "that the scriptures were being generally wrested and abused, contrary to their native tendency and proper drift and scope.[7]

Infant baptism rested on passages taken out of context, thereby providing a spurious basis for the practice. According to Patient this observation led him to understand other aspects of New England doctrine and practice to have depended upon the same method of biblical interpretation. Yet, despite these conclusions, Patient experienced internal conflict. The burgeoning conviction in Patient's mind was because it lay upon misconstrued and ill-applied Scripture, the standing order of Massachusetts was utterly corrupt. Specifically, the root cause of Massachusetts' societal debasement was infant baptism. However, fear of rejection and reprisal by church and society paralyzed him from publicly acting on this newly discovered truth.

The risks Patient faced were dire. Public dissent regarding infant baptism, and hence the Christian commonwealth intimately associated with it would incur excommunication, imprisonment, loss of property, and exile. Fear of such reprisals intensified Patient's turmoil, "as my evil and treacherous heart" resisted "the blessed motions of the Spirit of God."[8] Eventually Patient's angst subsided as he embraced the truth regarding infant baptism with increasing conviction. Even after the cessation of his spiritual crisis Patient further researched the

---

[7] Patient, *Doctrine of Baptism*, B.
[8] Patient, *Doctrine of Baptism*, B4.

question of infant baptism by listening to more sermons, and studying intensely the works of its advocates. These inquiries only confirmed Patient's conclusions regarding the invalidity of infant baptism. Shortly thereafter, Patient began publicly expressing his newly forged views. Patient's conflict with the New England order came to an impasse when he refused to have his son baptized, resulting in a summons to appear before the quarterly court in Essex, Massachusetts in June, 1633. Failure to resolve this dispute with the General Court soon necessitated Patient's departure from the colony. From there, he traveled to Virginia where his experience with the Anglican establishment there proved far worse than in Massachusetts. Needless to say, Patient did not linger long in Virginia.

After leaving Virginia, Patient traveled back north, but this time to South Jersey, where he ministered among the Cohansey Indians about a decade before John Eliot commenced his famous work among the Native Americans. Patient later returned to England in 1639, where he found a nation beset by significant political and ecclesiastical crises.

Patient arrived in England on the eve of the Civil War. As the war ensued, Patient involved himself in the administration of the Parliamentary forces under Cromwell. Shortly after his return to England, Patient met William Kiffin with whom he formed an abiding friendship. Patient went on to assist Kiffin in pastoring a Baptist congregation at Devonshire Square, London. Along with Kiffin, Patient signed the 1644 *London Confession of Faith*, as well as the 1646 and 1651 editions (though Patient had departed from London when the third edition was published). In 1645, Patient and Kiffin traveled throughout southeast England engaging in missionary work. However, their labors in Kent suffered reversal as they lost their converts to Arminian Baptists. Additionally, Patient entered the controversy with the Quakers, who denied the authority of Scripture, and instead appealed to the authority of an "inner light," as well as with the Ranters, who espoused a form of antinomianism.

In 1640 the ecclesiastical situation in Ireland was nothing less than dire. As a territory subject to England, Ireland was vulnerable to the ever-shifting policies of Tudor and Stuart monarchs. Throughout the Reformation, and specifically during the reigns of Elizabeth I (r.1558–1603) and James I (r.1603–1625), Protestantism largely served as a means of securing control of the predominantly Catholic population. Despite vigorous attempts to establish the Reformation in Ireland, such as the founding of Protestant Trinity College in Dublin in 1592, and the commissioning of learned, capable clergy, which included appointment of ardently Protestant bishops, these efforts ultimately proved unsuccessful as the majority of the Irish still, at least secretly, remained steadfastly Catholic. Moreover, the official Church of Ireland clearly manifested some glaring weaknesses such as clerical poverty, pluralism, and non-residence. Also many of the clergy were poorly educated and unable to speak Irish. Parliament was acutely aware of this severe state of affairs in the Irish Church, and earnestly desired to affect substantial reforms, but this would not occur until much later.

One of the complicating factors in the Irish situation facing Parliament was the form of ecclesiastical government best suited to the Church of Ireland. The two major options were a reformed Anglicanism or Presbyterianism. By 1647, both Parliament and the Protestant leaders of Ireland rejected Anglicanism with its government by episcopacy. Thus, the agenda at this point was to reconstitute the Irish Church as one with a Presbyterian polity. In the same year, Parliamentary forces gained control of Dublin. Afterwards, Parliament passed legislation that would impose a Presbyterian polity upon the Church of Ireland.

It was not until 1649 that the changes enacted by Parliament for dismantling the existing Church of Ireland were enforced, first in Dublin, and then throughout the rest of Ireland. This

"Rump" Parliament undertook the responsibility for arranging the logistics for continuing enforcement. Specifically, Parliament drew up an ordinance for the "propagation of the gospel" in Ireland. The ordinance passed Parliament on March 8, 1650. Prior to the ordinance's passage, Cromwell himself, along with the three chaplains, Hugh Peter (1598-1660), the theologian John Owen (1616-1683), and Jenkin Lloyd (b.1624), traveled to Ireland for the purpose of assessing the situation there so as to provide guided direction for implementing the ordinance.

As per the recommendation of the three chaplains, the Irish Ordinance mandated that six ministers be sent to Dublin. Moreover, the Ordinance required that generous salaries and other incentives be offered by the government to entice qualified ministers to move to Ireland and assist in the work of further reformation. One of the weaknesses of the Ordinance was that since Cromwell displaced Presbyterian hegemony by means of Pride's Purge,[9] and episcopacy had been outlawed, there had remained a significant religious vacuum to be filled in Ireland due to Cromwell's policy of religious toleration. This situation presented an unprecedented opportunity for Baptists.

The new religious environment fostered by Cromwell's policy through his governor of Ireland, Lord Deputy Fleetwood, hastened the increasing popularity of the Baptist movement which had initially been introduced into Ireland by English soldiers. Though himself an Independent, Fleetwood, because of his own commitment to religious freedom for the sake of freedom of conscience, afforded unrestricted freedom to Baptists to preach and teach throughout the country. However, even though Fleetwood's policy facilitated the spread of Baptist ideas throughout Ireland, it was not ultimately the cause of their

---

[9] On December 6, 1648, soldiers in Cromwell's New Model Army under the command Colonel Thomas Pride prevented Members of Parliament (MPs) opposed to this army from entering the House of Commons. Most of these hostile MPs were Presbyterians. The result of this was a significantly reduced legislative body known as the "Rump Parliament."

pervasive, national circulation, but rather the Baptist ministers themselves who moved from England to Ireland for the purpose of evangelism. Among these preachers the one likely to have exerted the most influence on the development of the Baptist movement in Ireland was Thomas Patient.

In March 1649, Parliament selected Patient as one of the six ministers who were to go to Dublin. Patient arrived at Kilkenny in April, 1650. By 1651 Patient had traveled to Waterford and Dublin, where he served as pastor of a local congregation. As a pastor, Patient conducted his ministry uncompromisingly on the basis of theological precision. This was especially the case in his opposition to mixed communion between Baptists and Independents at Christ Church Cathedral in Dublin. Facilitating this practice was Christ Church Cathedral's policy of open-membership on the basis of a profession of faith.[10] Patient stridently countered this approach to church membership and communion by insisting on a strict baptismal policy as prerequisite to participation in communion. Eventually, Patient's position prevailed, and he became pastor of Christ Church in Dublin. However, his tenure there soon ended with the erection of the first Baptist meetinghouse at Swift's Alley, Dublin of which Patient became pastor. Patient further augmented his pastoral work by representing the Dublin Baptists at the Waterford Conference in 1654. In same year, Patient published his only treatise, *The Doctrine of Baptism and the Distinction of the Covenants*, which is his substantial defense of credo-baptism.

Despite Patient's relative success in Ireland, times for Baptists would become difficult. The new governor, Henry Cromwell (1628–1674), wanted to limit the power of the military to which Baptists had close ties. For this reason, the governor was not friendlily disposed towards them. In the interest of removing power from the military, Cromwell attempted to regulate stringently even military affairs. Withdrawal of local

---

[10] Gazal, *Believer's Baptism in Cromwellian Ireland*, 17.

government support due to Cromwell's policies weakened the Baptist presence in Ireland. This waning of Baptist influence accelerated with the death of Lord Protector Cromwell, and the removal of his son, Richard from power for incompetence. By 1660, Baptists not only in Ireland, but throughout the rest of the British Isles, were a minority sect who hoped to obtain some degree of toleration from the new king, Charles II. Meanwhile Patient retained his position within the Baptist community as evident by the fact that his name headed a list of one hundred seventeen names affixed to the *Address from the Baptized Christians in Dublin* (1657), which attempted to show loyalty to Protector Cromwell. In 1659 Patient was still serving as chaplain to some military officers. Finally in 1660, the year of the Restoration, Patient returned to England, and served as assistant minister to Henry Hynam in Bristol, where in 1663 he was imprisoned for illegal preaching (as per the Clarendon Code) by Sir John Knight, the mayor. In 1666 Patient left for London, where once again he co-pastored with William Kiffin at Devonshire Square, the very place where his ministry as a Baptist began. Sadly, after only one month into his labors, Patient died of the plague, leaving his wife Sarah Patient, as his only survivor.

The Doctrine of Baptism and the Distinction of Covenants

Patient's only work, *The Doctrine of Baptism and the Distinction of Covenants*, truly stands as one of the most significant defenses of credo-baptism from a Reformed perspective. As a Particular Baptist, Patient subscribed generally to the same system of theology as Anglicans, Presbyterians, and Independents which emphasized human salvation as the result of God's unilateral and unconditional grace through the work of Jesus Christ within the framework of the Covenant of Grace. What makes this treatise by Patient distinct from other representative works of the early modern Reformed tradition is its defense of credo-baptism, and refutation of infant baptism by appropriating one of the central concepts of Reformed hermeneutics, the Covenant of Grace.

The majority of early modern Reformed theologians contended for infant baptism on the grounds that it replaced circumcision as the external sign and seal of the Covenant of Grace. Although these divines acknowledged that the New Testament neither gave any explicit command for Christians to baptize infants nor recorded any specific example of such practice having taken place, they nevertheless argued for the biblical warrant of the custom by employing the hermeneutic device of inference, or as Chapter 1 of the Presbyterian *Westminster Confession of Faith* describes it, interpreting Scripture "by good and necessary consequence." In applying this principle, Reformed advocates of infant baptism argued, since infants received an outward sign initiating them externally into the Covenant under its previous administration in ancient Israel, their counterparts under the gospel administration also obtained such a sign as a seal of their admission into the same Covenant with the only difference being that now the mark of initiation was water instead of circumcision, and that both boys and girls received it rather than the former only.

Patient predicates his defense of credo-baptism and critique of infant baptism upon his understanding of the Covenant of Grace as a spiritual covenant. As a spiritual covenant, the Covenant of Grace does not depend on an external sign and seal, but only faith for initiation into it. Conversely, Patient contends that other Reformed bodies bolster paedo-baptism with an erroneous understanding of the Covenant of Grace by insisting upon the necessity of entering into it by means of an external sign. Because it was a sign required of the ancient Israelites as part of their national covenant, circumcision pertained to the Covenant of Works, therefore making impossible any continuity with baptism as an external seal of the Covenant of Grace. This erroneous construal of the alleged continuity between circumcision and baptism, Patient contends, follows from excessive reliance on inference for biblical interpretation.

Throughout the treatise, Patient argues his thesis by stressing the four elements of New Testament baptism: the ministry, the form, the name in which one is to be baptized, and those who are to be baptized. Afterwards, Patient proceeds to refute extensively the sundry passages of Scripture advanced to support paedo-baptism by its proponents.

Patient's deft explanation of the Covenant of Grace as well as his thorough Scriptural exposition and clarity make *The Doctrine of Baptism and the Distinction of Covenants* arguably the definitive Reformed explication of the doctrine of credo-baptism. It argues fundamentally for an understanding of the Covenant of Grace whose administration is totally by grace alone as taught by Scripture alone. This work thus undeniably affirms the place of Particular Baptists in the broader Reformed family as ones who endeavored consistently to declare and practice the doctrines of grace. For these reasons, it is with joy that we re-introduce this seminal work to Reformed Baptist believers of the twenty-first century.

Features of this edition

This modern edition of *The Doctrine of Baptism and the Distinction of Covenants* is based on the 1654 text that was accessed through Early English Books Online. While retaining much of the original text, the spelling and some phrasing have been modernized. Moreover, the marginal headings have been moved to the body of the text as chapter headings and subheadings. Finally, there are footnotes that define archaic terms and provide background information so as to assist the reader in situating the text within its historical context.

Andre A. Gazal

Dedication

The epistle to the Christian reader, to whom the author witnesseth all grace and peace from God our Father through our Lord Jesus Christ

There being but a small moment of time from the Lord allotted to men in this life to run that Christian race set before them. And considering what Christ saith, "that whilst it is day, we ought to work, for the night cometh when no man can work."[11] And further considering, that Christ Jesus is gone to fetch a kingdom, and to return. He has left his servants several talents to be accounted for at his coming, when every man's award or punishment, shall be according to his works. This ought to provoke and stir up every Christian to a conscientious and careful improvement of his strength for God's glory and the service of his generation in this pilgrimage.

These, among many other motives, prevailed with me to present in this treatise to thy view, being also pressed thereunto by many of God's people, formerly in England, and late in Ireland.

Beloved reader, I know the world is filled with many books stuffed with very much of man's wisdom, which though the Apostle saith is "enmity with God;"[12] yet we find such discourses most pleasing to the carnal hearts of men in our age. Therefore, if that be the thing that thy itching ears do thirst after, thou mayest spare thyself that labor, for thou wilt find that with as much simplicity and plainness as possibly I could, I have

---

[11] John 9:4.
[12] James 4:4.

herein given out by clear Scripture-evidence, what the Lord hath made known to me.

For the clearing of this weighty point which God by his mighty power hath subjected my heart to believe, the which formerly by reason of my ignorance and error I was much averse unto.

For after it pleased God to reveal his Son in me, and to work a change in my heart, the great and weighty thing that God presented to me was, "to make my calling and election sure;" which I found to be a work filled with many difficulties, considering how far hypocrites might attain in the profession of godliness, and that they might come to have the counterfeit of all the grace in the child of God. And this the rather appeared more difficult because I found my own heart so desperately wicked and full of deceit, as Jeremiah 17:9 [says]. [I] also found the wiles and subtilties of the Devil, to be various, and I, constantly under several temptations, and deep desertions, when God (though for a little season) withdrew himself, and the light of his countenance from me, at which time I judged it my only thing necessary to prove whether Christ were in me, and my faith right as also my sincerity to the Lord. At which time I found but little settled rest or peace, till the Lord had put that great question out of doubt, in giving me a sure and well grounded confidence of my interest in him, till which time, I found little disposition on to search narrowly into other truths which I then thought to be too remote for me to exercise myself in, having received so much spiritual benefit, in communing with God and mine own heart, and searching out the difference betwixt the speaking of God's Spirit, my own spirit, and the spirit of Satan.

But when I came to some good measure of settlement in my confident and well grounded hopes, that I was the Lord's, then presently was I tempted, touching the main and material fundamental points in religion, which temptations, as they were a great cause of trouble and restlessness in my soul, so they

The Doctrine of Baptism

occasioned me with great eagerness, night and day, in use of the best means God presented to me, to seek satisfaction in the same, at which time the Lord did carry on my soul with much vehemencey after him, with much unweariedness.

For usually as one case and weighty question was answered to my satisfaction and comfort, another was stated in my soul too hard for me, in which experiences I for many years was exercised with all, in which time I was ignorant of the true way, which Christ would have his people to walk in.

But presently being convinced of the unwarentableness of the government of the Lordly Prelates, and the Liturgy in the Church of England, and the mixed communions in the parish assemblies,[13] I was resolved, God willing, to examine all religion as well in worship and the order of God's house, as I had done in other points. But I, at this time, being by the divine power of God, converted from the Church of England, though with great difficulty, being well furnished with arguments from pulpit and print, and divers able disputants for the defense of the false way; but God, breaking in by the power of his Spirit with clear Scripture-light, subjected my heart to the obedience of the truth, so that I found my heart closing with those truths in the love thereof.

At this time many godly Christians going to New England, and being come up in my judgement to the way of New England in faith and order, went over thither, being not convinced of my error, and great darkness in sprinkling the carnal seed of believers. But verily I thought, I had good warrant for that practice, having then in substance the same grounds for the defense thereof, that generally to this day is urged for the same. Yet having in my heart, so clear a light, discovering how shamefully in many things I had been deluded, and that by those which I could not but have charity to think were the Lord's own servants, and

---

[13] Patient here refers to the Church of England's government by episcopacy, and the *Book of Common Prayer* (1559).

finding the danger of receiving truths by tradition, was resolved to examine that point of baptism. And so I constantly resorted to the meetings of the people in New England, desiring to have good satisfaction in them, and their doctrine and practice, before I joined in communion. In order thereunto I constantly attended the preaching of the word, where hearing many, often preaching for baptizing of children of believing parents; I began to examine the grounds thereof, and the weight of their arguments, and genuine scope and drift of the scriptures, alleged by them to prove that point, and found that the scriptures were being generally wrested and abused, contrary to their native tendency and proper drift and scope. I also found, as I conceived, the foundation argument they urged was so exceeding contrary to several foundations of religion which both they and I did believe.

These things being hinted into my soul, I was resolved to examine the same, as I had formerly several other points of religion, with great profit and advantage. But upon this resolution temptations came in upon my heart urging that I was but weak, and in case it were not a truth, did I think so many men eminent for religion, piety, gifts and parts should not discover it sooner than I? Therefore, it was to no purpose for me to trouble myself. Unto which I had this answer in my soul, that I had been too long misled already on that ground, submitting to the liturgy, and that corrupt hierarchy.

Again, I considered that when the angels came with that message of glad tidings to all people, in Luke the second chapter, declaring the birth and nativity of Christ, the Lord then made the choice of the poor simple shepherds watching their flocks by night.

In the first place, this eminent truth was delivered and revealed to them when all learned and eminent men of Israel had no knowledge thereof.

And finding the poor thief on the cross to have sounder judgment than the General Synod or council of learned men at Jerusalem,[14] and also the speech of Christ to this purpose in Matthew 11:25 where Christ thanks his Father for hiding "these things from the wise and prudent and revealing them to babes and sucklings, out of his good pleasure, the spirit being the wind which bloweth when and where it listeth."

And also finding some of Christ's disciples, bearing testimony of Christ, in Luke 19:38, 39, 40. The Pharisees desired Christ to rebuke them; but Christ answered and said, "I tell you if these should hold their peace, the stones would immediately cry out." Here I observed Christ to descend and not to ascend. He does not say, if his simple and weak disciples should neglect their testimony, the learned Pharisees would cry out. He says, if his disciples neglect, the stones should cry out, which manifests that God loves to choose the most simple and foolish things by which to reveal his will.

And then, again, I found God not so much engaged by promise to reveal himself to men, considered of such outward and excellent parts, but in Psalm 25:14, "The secrets of the Lord are with them that fear him, and he will shew them his covenant." And Christ said in John 15:15, "You are my friends, if you do whatsoever I command you; henceforth I call you not servants, for the servant knoweth not what his Lord doeth; but I have called you friends, for all things that I have heard of the Father I have made known to you." And David saith, "Thou hast made me wiser than my teachers, because I have kept thy commandments." Here the Lord promises teaching principally to such as fear him and conscientiously keep his commandments, guiding them in judgment, and in the way that he should choose.

Notwithstanding, I found further objections in my heart, that though it was not men of parts, and outward learning,

---

[14] Acts 15:1–33.

but babes and sucklings, having their hearts bowed to obedience, and to the holy fear of God, that God would teach, yet I was sensible of so much evil in my heart that I questioned whether I might not be misled. Upon which I was put upon humble and fervent prayers to the Lord to guide and teach me, and to reveal his mind to me. Having again resolutions to seek the mind of God in this truth, and great encouragements to believe that God would satisfy me, and the rather from my former experience of His goodness having satisfied me in many weighty points that I was every way as much unsettled in.

Upon which this temptation came in afresh upon me, what need I trouble myself in a point so disputable, for if by my search and trial in that matter, I should come to see grounds swaying me in conscience against children's baptism that then I should be generally despised, and slighted of all the godly in that country, and not only be frustrated of communion and fellowship with them, but must also expect to suffer imprisonment, confiscation of goods, banishment at least, which would be my ruin, not knowing where to go, but in the woods amongst Indians, and wild beasts?[15]

Under this temptation I had a sore conflict, my evil and treacherous heart resisting the blessed motions of the Spirit of God, but considering that the ground of those discouraging arguments did arise from the flesh and the Devil, as Peter when he said, "Pity thyself, Master, this thing shall not be to thee," my resolution was as Christ saith, "Get thee behind me, Satan, thou savourest not the things of God."[16]

---

[15] This would have been the typical prospect of individuals banished from the Massachusetts Bay Colony for challenging the standing order as was the case with Roger Williams and Ann Hutchinson. Where the former was concerned, it was his encounter with native Americans, whose property rights he defended against the Massachusetts authorities, that led to his missionary work amongst them within the larger context of his establishing the colony of Providence (i.e. Rhode Island).

[16] Matthew 16:23-24.

The Doctrine of Baptism

Which put me in no small agony or conflict for some good space together, but it pleased the Lord to set that Scripture home upon my heart, "Buy the truth, sell it not,"[17] buy the truth at any rate, if truth cost me my life, I must buy it, though I might have all the favor and friendship in the world I must not sell it, this wrought in me a grounded and settled resolution, that I would seek after the mind of God, as well in suffering truths, as other, because Christ saith, "He that keeps the word of my patience, I will keep him in the hour of temptation." Apprehending these words to be of Christ's patience, he, embracing and practicing whereof would bring the cross (that is, contempt and hatred from all sorts of men), I found Christ said for this cause he was born, and came into the world, to bear witness to the truth, these things satisfied me, and that from the Lord, that I ought to make diligent search what his mind was in this point.

Hereupon I found the special presence of God with me, carrying out my heart to the Lord by faith and earnest prayer to be instructed and guided, all which time I was not acquainted with any that opposed christening children, and conversed only with such as for the practice. Finding my carnal part to desire satisfaction in infant baptism, but the more I conferred with, or heard any preach for it, the more was I convinced of the folly and ignorance of that judgment and practice, having heard one man preach fifteen sermons upon this subject, urging that in substance which many considerable authors had wrote.

I also searched many authors who wrote thereof night and day, with much attention, weighing and examining the grounds they urged many times breaking my sleep by watching in the night season. At the last, it pleased the Lord to reveal his mind to me, so that I was enlightened in my understanding to see answers to whatsoever I had heard. Here, the Lord breaking in with, not only a clear light in me, as to the matter in question, but three days, one after another, coming into my soul with

---

[17] Proverbs 23:23.

sealing manifestations of his love, and that with such scriptures so pertinent and suitable to my condition. There was a warrant at this time issued out to apprehend and bring me before the General Court in New England, which is no trouble to me. I am filled with unspeakable joy, as I have walked up and down in the woods in that wilderness, about my business. This discovery from God did much settle me in that truth which in substance thou wilt find in this treatise, upon which God wrought in me a true repentance, and sorrow of heart, that I had so long, both in opinion and practice, gone so sinful a way as I found that to be.

I have not in this treatise gone about to undertake a confutation of any one man, but upon my long experience in this subject matter, have taken up the main argument, which is the foundation that all the rest are grounded upon. I have bent my understanding in answer to that, which being overthrown, all other arguments fall with it.

Christian reader, I judge the clear evidence of Scripture light, which I do here give out to confirm the dipping believers,[18] will be sufficient to reprove all that darkness generally asserted in many large discourses about this point of christening children.

But further, that which I have had much in observation hath been a great deal of malice and contempt discovered from the devil against this truth.

First, in that the devil did by subtilties and fair pretenses in the first apostacy, sow this error in the minds of people, that this ordinance was of use to regenerate and convey grace, and to them who should be thought unfit to receive it, it had been a

---

[18] Originally a pejorative reference to their increasing use of immersion as the preferred mode of baptism as opposed to affusion (the pouring of water over the head of the person being baptized), Baptists like Patient will identify themselves as "Dipping Believers" as a means of distinguishing themselves from paedobaptists. An example of the derogatory use of this term is the title of Daniel Featley's anti-Baptist treatise, *The Dippers Dipt, or, the Anabaptists Duck'd and Plung'd over Head and Eares* (London: 1646).

The Doctrine of Baptism

great unmercifulness to the let children or any be without the same.

Thus that subtle enemy the Devil, destroys God's ordinances, and set up another of his own in the room thereof, which still remains upon the papists and generally all our carnal Protestants, both priests and people, concluding the dangerous estate of that child that dies unbaptized, therefore midwives on this ground were tolerated to baptize if a child were like to die, putting a value thereon, as if it had conveyed grace.

But many good men have renounced this, though the devil hath showed his malice in blinding them still to practice the same evil, though upon another ground lately found out, and that is the subject this book opposeth. Others see the darkness and error of christening carnal children upon any ground, but the devil shows his rage against that ordinance in them, that rather than they will embrace it as from the Lord, contradict and oppose the same, saying,

> There is no ordinance or church to be found in the world. His malice also appears in such as boast of their being above ordinances, saying, that Christ and ordinances are at end, that dispensation being for that time or age, but now they have Christ in Spirit, the substance being come, the shadows vanish.[19]

Thus the devil strangely appears like himself as if he had forgot his language in the papist and carnal Protestant, that this ordinance regenerated in the very work done,[20] and that the salvation or damnation depended upon it. When now in others, what

---

[19] Patient refers to the Quakers who rejected outward sacraments as relics of the Old Covenant that was replaced by a purely inward worship instituted by Christ.

[20] Reference to the Roman Catholic idea of *ex opera operato* (Literally, "Out of the work worked), wherein the sacrament, which in this case is baptism, conveys grace when performed. The fact that Patient attributes this understanding to both the Roman Catholic and Protestant views of baptism implies that he conceived of them as holding to some form of baptismal regeneration.

is washing or dipping in a little water, but a low or legal thing? So that if the devil's delusions and inventions are not closed withal, then Christ's ordinances are vilified and condemned.

And further, Satan manifests his malice in throwing contempt upon the obedient and upright practicers of the same, to raise prejudices from a story of what strange creatures were of that opinion at Munster in Germany,[21] and stirs up others to pry into the dark side of the saints, I mean their personal frailties, "As the Egyptian in the Red Sea, to their own destructions, the cloud was darkness to them, but gave light to the Israelites" (Exod. 14:20). The Egyptians' eyes were only on the black or dark side of the cloud; therefore, they stumbled and fell, but the Israelites had the light part thereof for the safety, which is compared to the conversation of the saints (Heb. 12:1) where there is a light part, their graces and virtues, but their dark part is their failings, which malice or prejudice will not suffer many men to see beyond. "For a man that hates his brother walks in darkness" as John saith. The tempter accused Job, that he did not serve God for nought, he was hedged about, God had preferred him to honor and riches and place of authority in the world, as appears in Job 29 which malice he now a days manifesteth against the prosperity of his saints, desiring to stain their holy obedience with improbrious language of self-seeking and preferment. When the professors of this truth have been the persons ordinarily stoned, and suffering the violence of the multitudes where they have not been protected by godly magistrates.

Christian friend, do not read this book with a heart prejudiced against the same for the sake of the instrument or

---

[21] Patient alludes to the infamous episode of 1534 in which a fringe Anabaptist group led by Jan van Leiden and Bernard Rothmann took over the city of Munster, and proclaimed it the "New Jerusalem." Claiming to receive visions, van Leiden proclaimed himself King of Munster, and decreed the mandatory execution of "the godless." Moreover, he instituted polygamy, and ordered all property to be held in common. In June 1535, Catholic and Protestant forces retook Munster, and slaughtered almost all of the inhabitants along with van Leiden and Rothmann.

plainness of the style; it was not intended to please men, but in faithfulness to discharge a duty to God from whom I received what I have laid before thee, and to answer the of many Christians, which have been for some years past neglected, through my indisposedness to this work. However, if thou shalt by this my weak endeavor reap any satisfaction of edification in the truth, let God the author of every good and perfect gift have the praise, which is only due to him, and not his

Unworthy Servant,
Thomas Patient

Acts 2:37–38

Now when they heard this, they were pricked in their hearts, and said unto Peter *and the rest of the Apostles, Men and Brethren what shall we do?*

Then Peter *said unto them, Repent and be baptized everyone of you in the name of Jesus Christ for the Remission of sins, and you shall receive the Gift of the Holy Ghost.*

1
The Occasion of the Words in the Text: Acts 2:37–38 Laid Open

These words of my text have a special dependence foregoing in the chapter; for in the beginning of the chapter you shall find that the apostles and the Church were with one accord in one place when the day of Pentecost was fully come, and according to the promise that Jesus Christ commanded them, to wait for, and that John had foretold of, "That one should come after him, that should baptize with the Holy Ghost, and with fire," the which was at this time fulfilled. The author of the Acts here relates, "Suddenly there came a sound from heaven as of a rushing, mighty wind, and it filled all the house where they were sitting, and there appeared unto them cloven tongues, like as of fire, and it sat upon each of them, and they were all filled with the Holy Ghost, and began to speak with other tongues as the Spirit gave them utterance."

Now this I understand to be the baptism which John speaks of viz. that of the Holy Ghost, and of fire, which Christ should dispense, as you may see was extraordinary, and upon special occasion communicated to the apostles, they being now to give testimony of Christ's death, resurrection, and ascension. The Lord in order to [perform] this work communicates to them the extraordinary gifts of the Holy Ghost, and that in an extraordinary manner. For here was outward signs, which were cloven tongues of fire resting on them; and here was also the Holy Ghost with the extraordinary effects of it, as the inward things signified by the outward sign, all which was (I understand) extraordinary, for the fitting of these apostles that extraordinary work which God had to do by them.

The reason why the Holy Spirit descended in an extraordinary manner upon the apostles

First, they were to be eye-witnesses of Christ's majesty in the flesh.

Secondly, they were to be master-builders to lay a foundation which all after ministers to the end of the world, were to build on, they being penmen of Scripture.

Thirdly, they were now to overthrow all the Jewish worship, and all the Mosaical administrations, put to an end by Christ's death, and to furnish them to this extraordinary work which Christ, as an effect of his session at the right hand of God, pours down the gifts upon them, as before mentioned. This being noised abroad, how they spake with other tongues, the multitude came together, wondering at them, and some thought they had been drunk, but Peter, standing up with the eleven, began to lift up his voice to teach them.

The content of Peter's sermon to the Jews upon the descent of the Holy Spirit

And first he proves by Scripture that these gifts of the Holy Ghost were formerly promised by the Lord, and, as an effect of his ascension, now given to them; and he endeavors in this sermon preached to prove,

First, that Jesus was the Christ, a man approved of God by miracles and signs, that God did work by him, amongst them.

Secondly, he endeavors to prove by Scripture, that he did suffer and die according to the counsel and will of God.

Thirdly, that he did rise again from the dead, which he from Scripture doth justify.

And that in the fourth place, God had exalted him "by his right hand to be both Lord and Christ," and proves that, by the visible gifts of the Holy Ghost, which they did see and hear, and lest they should not understand who he meant, he tells them in the verse before my text, "That it was the same Jesus which they had crucified, that God had made Lord and Christ. Now when they heard this, they were pricked in their hearts, and said unto Peter, and to the rest of the apostles, 'Men and brethren, what shall we do?'"

The benefit of preaching the Gospel
Whence observe from the text, that preaching and hearing the Gospel preached, is a special means to convert souls, as appears when Peter preached and clearly held forth, that he whom they had crucified and slain was now to be Lord and Judge, and exalted to that dignity by God the Father. When they heard this they were pricked in their hearts.

The beginning of true conversion
In the second place, we may observe from hence, that true conversion begins with a prick in the heart.

Thirdly, they, when wrought upon and pricked in their hearts, said to Peter, and to the rest of the apostles, "Men and brethren what shall we do?"

How they that begin to receive the saving life both towards it and them that hold it forth
Whence in the third place observe, that it is the disposition of such that have the beginning of saving light, to desire more, and that from them whom God hath spoken to their souls by.

Obedience accompanieth true conversion
Fourthly, that which they do earnestly enquire after is, what shall we do which respecteth obedience; they believing Christ to be a Lord as well as a Savior, know that he must be submitted to, therefore said they, "What shall we do?"

All called to repentance by the Gospel
Whence we observe, that a true converted soul is an obedient soul.

In verse 38 the answer of Peter to them is in these words, "Repent, and be baptized everyone of you," from whence we do observe further, that where the Gospel is preached, all men are called to repent.

Whoever believes and repents ought to be baptized
Lastly, that it is the duty of every man that believes and repents to be baptized.

Now this last observation of the text is that which I shall at present speak to for the satisfaction of such souls that may at present be doubtful of this truth, and for confirming such souls as do already believe it.

2
The Ordinance of Baptism Explained and the Four Elements of Baptism

Now for the better and more clear speaking to this point in hand I shall explain what his ordinance of baptism is. And that in four things which will more clearly appear if we examine the commission that Christ gives his disciples in Matthew 28:19-20 where we find [in] v.15 that the eleven disciples were sent by Christ, who hath all power in heaven and earth given to him (v.18 & v.19). Christ saith, "Go ye therefore and teach all nations, baptizing them in the name of the Father, Son, and Holy Ghost, teaching them to observe whatsoever I have commanded you," from whence you may observe four things contained in this commission essential to this ordinance of baptism. Here is the first ministry, secondly the form, thirdly the name into which, and fourthly the subjects.

Who is a lawful minister of baptism

First, the ministers that must dispense this ordinance, and this preaching disciples, and so in the 16th verse are the eleven denominated, then the eleven disciples went away into Galilee, and Jesus (in verse 18) came and spake unto them, saying, "All power is given unto me in heaven, and earth; Go ye therefore and teach all nations baptizing them."

Whence you may observe, that the persons bid to go are disciples enabled to teach the doctrine of the Gospel for the conversion of souls to faith, and repentance; for it is clear, That they are bid to teach, are bid to baptize also; so that from this commission I gather, that a disciple enabled to bring down God to a soul, and to bring a soul again up to God, is a lawful minister of baptism; for that is the tenor of the New Covenant (Heb. 8:10). "I will be to them a God, and they shall be to me a people;

and I am my beloved's and my beloved is mine" (Song of Sg. 6:3), so that as God in Christ is to be opened, and that in all the fundamental doctrines of faith, for man's salvation, so is the soul's conformity to God to be preached, as the soul's conformity to God to be preached, as the soul's duty to God again. Where God hath furnished a minister with abilities from himself to declare the doctrine of faith and repentance, to conversion, and having converted that soul, it is furnished with the knowledge of God to teach to this soul all the fundamental ordinances according to the commission which saith, "Teaching them to observe whatsoever I have commanded you." It is without doubt that this is a justifiable minister sent from the Lord according to the commission. But though a man should be able to preach the doctrine of faith, and that ably for the conversion of souls unto that faith, yet being destitute of the true knowledge of the doctrine of baptism, and how it ought to be dispensed. To be sure, this man is not a justifiable minister according to the commission, that when he hath converted souls to the faith, neither knows how to discover to these men the fundamental ordinances of God, neither can discover to them the evil of those superstitious practices, they have been nursed up in by the traditions of their fathers.

Yet notwithstanding I dare not say, but so far as they have a gift, they are warranted to administer the same from the first of Peter 4:10, [which] saith, "Let everyone as he hath received the gift minister," and so it was thought lawful for any Christian man in that sense to administer such gifts which God hath bestowed on them.

But sure it is that these that are utterly unacquainted how to dispense the ordinance of baptism, were never sent of God to dispense it, that instead of dipping do sprinkle, and instead of the true subject a believer, dispense it upon a carnal, ignorant child; and instead of doing it into the name of Father, Son, and

The Doctrine of Baptism

Holy Ghost, do sprinkle them at the naming of so many words only.

The true form of baptism

In the second place, the true form of baptism is commanded of the Lord Jesus by way of dipping, and, as it were, by drowning, overwhelming, or burying in water, and not by sprinkling with water, as appears many ways.

First, in that although there be frequent mention made of that appointment of Christ, in his last will and testament, yet it is never expressed in the word, that may be rendered "rantism,"[22] or sprinkling, but by the word that is rendered "baptism," or "dipping."

Secondly, in that the word by which it is so frequently expressed, doth in proper English signify to "dip," "to plunge under water," and as it were, to drown them, so as with safety the party (as to the manner) may be drowned again and again.

See in the instance of Naaman, who dipped himself seven times in Jordan (2 Kings 5:14). To this sense of the word (at least in this place) both the Greek, Latin, and English churches agree, as is affirmed by able authors.

Thirdly, in that the phrase in which there is mention made of such an appointment of Christ is affirmed, doth necessarily import such a thing; and therefore when mention is made of baptizing, which is commonly translated "in," or "into," suits with dipping, and not that preposition which signifies "with," and so suits with sprinkling.

And therefore it may be as well rendered, "I baptize you in water, and he shall baptize you in the Holy Spirit" (Mark 1:8). So it is rendered, John did baptize in the wilderness, and in the River of Jordan (v.4, 5), or that John was in the Spirit on the Lord's Day, Revelation 1:10. And they were baptized in the

---

[22] ["Rantism," a condition characterized by ranting. Patient obviously uses the word sarcastically in relation to the arguments of paedo-baptists].

Cloud, and in the sea (1 Cor. 10 and 7). It may as well be rendered, "I baptize you, or dip you into water, as it is rendered, they were casting a net into the sea (Mark 1:16), for which words are affirmed to be the same, and it would be too improper of speech to say, "John did baptize with the wilderness," and "they were casting a net with the sea."

Fourthly, that this appointment of Christ is, by way of dipping, and not sprinkling, appears.

In that for the resemblance and likeness hereunto the Israelites, passing under the cloud, and in the sea, where the Egyptians, that were lords and commanders, their pursuers and enemies, that sought their destruction, were drowned, left behind, and seen no more, is by the Holy Spirit, called a "baptism" (1 Cor. 10:2). They were baptized in the cloud.

Where observe, it is not here rendered "with the cloud," and "with the sea," as in the other place (Mark 1:8), "with water," because it suits with sprinkling, although the word be the same. But "in the cloud," and "in the sea," which suits with "dipping," or "overwhelming," and so with the appointment of Christ. They, passing through the midst of the Red or Bloody Sea on dry land, which stood on both sides as a wall, and being under the cloud as men (in a carnal eye), overwhelmed and drowned, and yet truly saved, and safe from their enemies.

Fifthly, that this appointment of Christ was not by sprinkling, but by dipping or putting the person into, or under water, appears by Philip's baptizing the eunuch, that was the person, to be baptized; and being there in the water, Philip baptized or dipped him in that water, as John did Jesus in the River of Jordan.

And it is said, They descended, or went down into the water, so they ascended or went straight way up, or out of the water, (Acts 8:38-39; Matt. 3:16). Mark the expression, "And Jesus, when he was baptized went up straightway out of the Water," therefore he had been down in the water.

The Doctrine of Baptism

Sixthly, that this appointment of Christ, was not by sprinkling, but by dipping, or as it were, a drowning, appears, that John the Baptizer (his work being to baptize) remains in the wilderness by the River of Jordan, and afterwards in Enon, near Salem, and the reason that is rendered, by the Spirit of the Lord, why he abode there, was, because there was much water, which need not have been, if that appointment could have been performed by sprinkling and not by dipping (See Luke 3:2-3; John 3:8; 1:23).

Seventhly, that this appointment of Christ was not to be performed by sprinkling, but by dipping, appears from the nature of the ordinance itself; for it is such an ordinance as whereby the person that submitteth thereto, doth visibly put on Christ Jesus the Lord, and is hereby visibly planted into his death, holding forth therein a lively similitude and likeness unto his death, whereby only through faith, he now professeth he hath escaped death, and is in hopes to obtain life everlasting, and so to have fellowship with him in his death, and to reckon himself dead with him to sin, Satan, the Law, and the curse (See Gal. 3:27; Rom. 6:2-3, 5-7, 9; 1 Cor.15:29).

But the planting of a person into the likeness of death is no way resembled by sprinkling, but by dipping, it is lively set forth and demonstrated.

Eighthly, this appointment of Christ's baptism is an ordinance whereby the person that submitteth thereto, doth hereby visibly and clearly resemble the burial of Christ, and his being buried, in respect of the old man, the former lusts and corruptions (like the Egyptians) to be taken away and seen no more (See Rom. 6:4, 6; Col. 2:12). But sprinkling doth no way lively resemble the burial of Christ, or the person being buried with him as dipping doth

Ninthly, this appointment of Christ's baptism is an ordinance, whereby the person that submitteth thereto, doth visibly and lively hold forth herein the resurrection of Christ, declares him whose life was taken away from the earth, to be alive again, who although he died and was buried, yet was not left in the grave to see corruption, but was raised again, and behold he liveth forevermore.

And as hereby he holds forth the resurrection of Christ, so doth also his own, being planted in the likeness thereof, so as to reckon himself to be in soul and spirit, quickened and risen with Christ, from henceforth to live unto God, the fountain of life, and Christ Jesus the Lord, who died for him, and rose again, and so to walk in the newness of life in this present world, being also begot into a lively hope, that in the world to come, he shall be raised and quickened both in soul and body, to a life everlasting (See Rom. 6:4-5, 8, 11; Acts 8:33, 35-36; Col. 2:13; 1 Cor. 15:29; 1 Peter 1:3).

But sprinkling doth no way lively resemble the resurrection of Christ, or the soul or bodies rising, or being raised by him, as the way of dipping doth.

Therefore this appointment of Christ, was and still is to be performed by way of dipping or putting the person into, or under the water, and not by sprinkling.

Tenthly, dipping doth hold forth a conformity to Christ in his sufferings and afflictions, as Christ saith, "I have a baptism; and how am I straightened until it be accomplished,"[23] meaning his sufferings.

Now one end of baptism is to represent Christ's sufferings, and our sufferings with him, which is in a lively manner set out by dipping into water, and therefore when the saints do express their afflictions, they do set them forth by being in the depths, or in the deep waters, as David in Psalm 130, "Out of the depths I have cried unto the Lord," meaning deep afflictions, and God saith in Isaiah 43:2, "When thou passest through the waters, they shall not overflow thee," meaning affliction, and therefore a believer, is to be dipped and plunged, all over into the river or

---

[23] Luke 12:50.

water, to hold forth. That now he must resolve to take up the cross of Christ and suffer, and not only so, but this being raised and delivered out of the water again by the hands of the minister, doth hold forth that so shall such believing souls be saved, and delivered from all their afflictions, as in Psalm 34:17: "Many are the afflictions of the righteous, but God shall deliver them out of all."

And that this doth sign or signify our salvation, appears in 1 Peter 3:21, the like figure whereunto baptism doth now save us. And in Mark 16:16: "He that believes and is baptized shall be saved." So that baptism is to sign, and to confirm signally, our sufferings and afflictions with Christ, so salvation or deliverance from them all, the one in dipping and plunging him in water, the other in raising him out again.

Into whose name is baptism ministered

The third thing that is essential in this ordinance of baptism, which I shall speak to, will be what is meant by name of Father, Son, and Holy Ghost. The command is, that the minister must dip them into the name of the Father, Son, and Holy Ghost, the which the Lord Jesus commanding must be therefore essential to this ordinance, I shall therefore endeavor to shew you what is meant by "name" here.

That by which Father, Son, and Spirit are made known, as a man is by his name, that is hereto be understood, by the name Father, Son, and Holy Ghost, we know the Gospel doth hold forth one God, yet distinguished into Father, Son, and Holy Ghost, the name here is to be understood, that Gospel that doth so set forth God and describe him as the subject matter of our Faith (Acts 9:15). "But the Lord said unto Ananias, Go thy way, for he is a chosen vessel unto me, to bear my name before the Gentiles, and kings, and children of Israel, for I will shew him how great things he must suffer for my name's sake."

Now "name" in this place, and in the commission is to be understood, that heavenly mystery of the Gospel, in which God is discovered and made known, as a man by his name.

One part of the Gospel mystery consists of a discovery of the name of the Father, by which he is distinguishably made known from the Son and Spirit, and that in these particulars.

First, in ordaining the Son (Isa. 28:16, with 1 Pet. 2:5), in sending the Son (Gal. 4:4, John 3:16, 17), in sealing the Son (John 6:27), in promising the Son (Isa. 9:6), in bruising the Son and putting him to grief (Isa. 53), and laying all our iniquities upon the Son, and to justify and freely accept such as believe in the Son. This I understand is the name of the Father.

And by the Son's name is to be understood that by which he makes known himself to the sons and daughters of man, as to take flesh (Heb. 2:14; Rom. 9:5, 13). He kept the law in order to die as that just one, or as a lamb without spot, and his making his soul an offering for sin, as a perfect offering for the sins and transgressions of this people (Heb. 10:12, 14; Isa. 53). He did not only die for our sins, but rose again for our justification, ascended into heaven, and makes intercession for us (Rom. 4:25; Heb. 2:25). And pours down the Spirit and gives gifts unto men, (Zech. 12:10; Eph. 4:10-12). All this the Son makes himself known by as by a name, distinguishably from the Father, and the Spirit.

And in the last place, the Spirit is made known in the Gospel, as that which in the first place convinceth the world of sin, John 16:8 and pricks men in their hearts with a sense of sin, and the wrath of God due for sin (Acts 2:37, 29). And the work of the Spirit, by which that is made known, is the revealing of the Father, and the Son, and those great mysteries unto the soul of a poor convicted sinner, for as Christ saith, "The Spirit of God shall lead you into all truth. It shall take of mine, and shew it to you" (John 16), and so man doth understand, "the things of God, but by the Spirit of God; for the Spirit of God searcheth

The Doctrine of Baptism

out all things, even the deep things of God" (1 Cor. 2:9-10). The Spirit doth not only discover man's misery, and his lost estate by reason of sin, but discovers a remedy which lies in the great love of God in Christ (as before mentioned) and worketh in the heart, true faith and repentance, disposing the heart to obedience. This is the proper work or office of the Spirit, by which he is distinguishably known from the Father and the Son.

And now, when the soul shall come to the preacher, and make known to him that the Spirit hath experimentally made known unto him his lost and damnable estate by sin, and that [t]he same Spirit hath discovered unto him the great love of God the Father, in the gift of Christ, to be a propitiation for sin, as dying for the chief of sinners, and that the Spirit of God hath made known all this to him, and hath wrought faith in his heart to believe it, and hath changed his heart from a course of sin to renewed obedience; for no soul can declare to a minister the true work of conversion, but he must in so doing discover his knowledge of the work of the Father, Son, and Spirit, and into this doth the minister baptize him, as in the name of the Father, Son, and Holy Ghost. And thus much for these particulars.

The subject of baptism

In the fourth place, we shall now come to the subject that must be baptized, and that (as you have heard) is one that is taught, "Teach all nations, baptizing them;" and as my text saith, "Repent, and be baptized every one of you," which doth hold forth the person baptized to be a taught and repentant person.

But seeing the main thing in question hath always seemed to be the subject of baptism, who it is that is to be baptized; this I shall therefore most insist upon, wherein I shall endeavor to make plain to you first (I say) that he is to be a believer, a penitent person, as appears [in] Mark 26:26: "Go preach the Gospel to every creature, he that believeth, and is baptized shall be saved."

3
Faith and Repentance Go Before Baptism

That believing the Gospel is to go before baptizing, and Matthew 28:19: "Teach all nations, baptizing (or dipping) them." What [is] "them?" "Them" that are taught or made disciples by teaching, and in my text you find that Peter, after Christ had poured down the Spirit upon them doth (by that authority received from heaven), when he had converted those Jews, command every one of them, to be baptized or dipped. "Repent and be baptized, every one of you, into the name of the Lord Jesus for the remission of sins,"[24] and so in like manner you shall find Cornelius, his family, by Peter commanded to be baptized, Acts 10:48. For saith he to the six brethren that were with him, "How shall we forbid water that these should not be baptized, who have received the Holy Ghost, as well as we?"

And he, by the great authority which (as an extraordinary apostle) he had from heaven, commanded them to be baptized in the name of the Lord Jesus. So we find Ananias in a special manner sent to the Apostle Paul at his first conversion to the faith, as [in] Acts 22:16, where he also by the authority received from Christ in verse the 16th saith, "And now Paul why tarriest thou? Arise and be baptized, for the washing away of thy sins in calling upon the name of the Lord," where you see the express command of God, enjoining him (upon his conversion) to be baptized.

And in the next place, as God hath commanded his ministers to baptize or dip believers only, and as ministers (by virtue of that authority from him) have left standing laws, and commands upon disciples only to be baptized, so we find that they did practice that way and only, of baptizing such as believed and repented (Acts 2:40–42): "So many as gladly received the word,

---

[24] Acts 2:38.

were baptized, and the same day there were added to the Church, three thousand souls. And they continued in the apostles' doctrine, fellowship, breaking of bread, and prayer."

Whence you may observe the practice of the apostles that were guided by the infallible gifts of the Spirit, that first they converted before they baptized.

In like manner you shall find in Acts 8:12-13, where Philip was preaching to the people in Samaria. But when they believed (he preaching the things concerning the Kingdom of God, the name of Jesus Christ), they were baptized, both men and women. Then Simon himself believed also; and when he was baptized he continued with Philip and wondered. So that you see this was the continued course of Christ's messengers sent by him.

First, they converted men by preaching, and then baptized them in the name of the Lord Jesus, wherein the name of the Father and Spirit are included, when his name is only mentioned. In like manner you shall find in the same chap[ter] that Philip was directed, by the Spirit of the Lord, to the eunuch that did belong to Candace, the Queen of the Ethiopians, who had the charge of all her treasure, and had been at Jerusalem for to worship, was returning, and reading Isaiah the prophet. Philip joined himself to the chariot, and upon some discourse together, he, from the aforesaid Scripture, preached unto him Jesus, in Acts 8:32, &c.

> And as they went on their way they came to a certain water, and the Eunuch said, "See, here is water, what hindereth me to be baptized?" Philip said, "If thou believest with all thy heart, it is lawful" (implying it was unlawful for a man not believing to be baptized). And he answered and said, "I believe that Jesus Christ is the Son of God," and he commanded the chariot to stand still, and they went both down into the water, both Philip and the eunuch, and he baptized him, and when they were come out of the water, the Spirit of the Lord caught away Philip

The Doctrine of Baptism

that the eunuch saw him no more, and he went his way rejoicing.

Believers should offer themselves to be baptized

From all these words you may observe, that Philip is said to preach Christ unto this man, and upon his coming to the water he said, "What lets?" where you see, it is the duty of such as believe to offer themselves to be baptized, and that there is no let or hinderance to the ordinance of baptism but unbelief, and therefore saith he, "If thou believest with all thy heart, thou mayest" (or it is lawful as the word more properly may be read), plainly holding forth, that all, both young and old, that did not believe, it was unlawful for them to be baptized.

And you shall find several families also baptized upon their being converted, which many (through ignorance and want of taking notice of what the Scripture speaks) say, it is probable they had some infants in them.

Lydia and her household converted

But to prevent mistakes in the minds of any that so think, I shall prove that these families were all converted disciples so as to believe the Gospel, as for instance, first, the family of Lydia (Acts 15:14-15): "And a certain woman named Lydia, a seller of purple, of the city Thyatira (which worshiped God) heard us, whose heart the Lord opened, that she attended to the things which were spoken of Paul, and when she was baptized, she besought us, saying, If ye judge me faithful to the Lord, come into my house and abide, and she constrained us."

Now here in this text, Lydia is only mentioned as to have been converted, no mention made what her household was, only that they were baptized, but in the last verse, viz. the 40th of that chapter, it is said that when Paul and Silas, were put out of the gaoler's house, they went and entered into the house of Lydia, and when they had seen the brethren, they comforted them and departed, where you may clearly see that Lydia's house consisted of brethren capable of being visited and comforted by Paul and Silas as well as Lydia, whose household they were.

The Gaoler and his household together converted
And also in the same chapter you have mention made of the Gaoler and his household, all which were baptized in the 31st, 32nd, 33rd, and 34th verses, in which place you shall, upon reading, find this to be true, that they spake unto him the word of the Lord, and to all that were in his house, and verse 34: "He set meat before them, and rejoiced, believing in God with all his house."

Where it is plain that the whole household of the gaoler heard the word of God, and rejoiced, and believed as well as the gaoler, and were all baptized, which is clear proof that such hearing the word of God, and believing ought and they only, to be baptized.

Stephanus and his household together converted
And this will appear further by the house of Stephanus, comparing 1 Corinthians 11:6 with the 16th chapter and the 15th verse of the same epistle, where in the one place it is said that Paul baptized the household of Stephanus, in the last place he speaketh thus, "I beseech you, brethren, ye know the house of Stephanus, that it is the first fruits of Achaia, and that they have addicted themselves to the ministry of the saints, that you submit yourselves unto such, and to everyone that helpeth with us and laboreth."

Where you see in one and the same epistle (as he saith) he baptizeth this household so he affirms they were the first fruits of Achaia, and that they were ministers, and addicted themselves to the ministering unto the saints, they did as the text notes, labour, and he would have the Church submit themselves

The Doctrine of Baptism

unto such, therefore they were not babes, or little infant, but all true converts, believing and penitent persons.

And in Acts 18:8, for the further clearing of this matter in hand, "And Crispus, the chief ruler of the synagogue, believed on the Lord with all his house, and many of the Corinthians believed, and were baptized": So that you see what a catalogue of clear examples you have to confirm unto us, which way those infallible apostles, both taught and practiced, according to the great commission given them, by the authority of Christ from heaven, to preach first the Gospel to every creature, and he that believeth and is baptized, should be saved, and that they should make disciples through teaching, dipping them into the name of the Father, Son, and Holy Ghost; And withal you see both commands as you have heard, and plentiful examples for baptizing believers. But not the least colour or shew of any ground for sprinkling infants.

Now by the way, let me say, what a sad thing therefore is this, that such a world of people (from custom and tradition) run headlong after this idol of man's invention?

But this solemn ordinance, which you have heard, lies clearly as a duty under the express law of Christ to everyone that believeth, this they slight and condemn as enemies of the same. Therefore, let such souls know that as Christ is a king, so this is one of his great laws, and a fundamental ordinance of the Gospel unto which he calls all believing and penitent persons, that are professed subject to him be obedient to.

4
The Ordinance of Baptism Long Neglected, and an Idol Set in Its Room

Now therefore let such tender souls who have the fear of God in them lay this to heart.

First, that this solemn ordinance for many hundred years hath been neither preached nor practiced, by abundance of such which (in charity) we cannot but judge might have many good things found in them.

But here lies that which makes the case sad and lamentable, that in the room of this precious ordinance of God (which Christ confirmed by his blood) should be set up, that idol of sprinkling of carnal poor infants, for doubtless, if there be an idol now practiced in the world, or set up amongst men, this must needs be one. For I have learned with others of the saints of God this to be an idol, either the worshiping of a false God, or the true God in a false manner, which I might largely insist upon to prove from Scripture.

Now though this be not an idol for the first kind, it is without doubt an idol of the second. It is setting up man's invention instead of God's solemn ordinance, which is a sin for which God plagued the people in Leviticus 10 and 1, 2. It is an image of true baptism set up in the room of it, but not the same, and that in all the before mentioned essentials, a false administrator, ignorant of the true nature of the ordinance instead of a true minister; sprinkling instead of dipping; a carnal infant instead of a true believing man or woman. And all this done at the naming of so many words only. Whereas the commission enjoins that they should dip them in the name of the Father, Son, and Holy Ghost. So that there is in this christening of children nothing of God's appointment or what he commanded, viz. the minister wrong, the subject wrong. The form wrong, and also the naming of so many words only instead of dipping into the name of the Father, Son, and Holy Ghost, whereas the commission enjoins the true minister should dip a disciple into the name of Father, Son, and Holy Ghost.

The papists hold that the ordinance of baptism conveyeth grace by the very work done
Now let any soul seriously judge whether God can own that which hath nothing of his own appointment or commands, but in every particular contrary thereunto.

But seeing the main thing usually controverted is about the subject (whether infant or believer), I shall leave what I have said, concluding the administration upon children corrupt in all the three foresaid heads as well as in the last, and shall speak of the last only, viz. that carnal children are not lawful subjects of baptism. I shall begin to speak to the main argument or ground, usually pleaded by all, except Papists,[25] for children's baptism, and that is,

Though there be no command nor example, yet there is a consequence, viz. the covenant of life being made to believers, and their seed coming out of their loins, baptism, being an ordinance of the covenant, doth also belong to them.[26]

---

[25] T.P.: The Papists hold that the ordinance of baptism doth convey grace by the very work done [*ex opera operato*], which is so generally confuted by all Protestant authors, that I think it not worth my time to speak to that gross error.

[26] Though implied by the Thirty-Nine Articles (# VI, XXVII), and the Book of Common Prayer, the hermeneutical device of formulating doctrine on the basis of inference drawn from the alleged preponderance of Scriptural teaching is explicitly affirmed by the Westminster Confession of Faith, Chapter 1, paragraph 8: "The whole counsel of God concerning all things necessary for His own glory, man's salvation, faith and life, is either expressly set down in Scripture, *or by good and necessary consequence may be deduced from Scripture*"[italics added]. It is this interpretive method that Patient seeks to impeach as the hermeneutical grounds for infant baptism.

Baptism of infants drawn by false consequence

Now I shall endeavor to prove the falseness and erroneousness of this consequence.[27] That it cannot be of God, my first ground is, because it doth oppose itself to the express laws and commands of the New Testament. Whatsoever consequence men do draw from Scripture, that crosseth the plain commands of God (to be sure) cannot be of God, but such consequence must needs be (according to Scripture light) of Satan, or at the best, from the vision of man's own heart.

Now this I would have you seriously to take notice of, that baptism of believers is a solemn ordinance of the New Testament, enjoined by divers special commands, and encouraged with promises of remission of sins and salvation on the right performance of the same.

Now for any man to force a consequence that shall oppose itself against so solemn an ordinance cannot be of God because God cannot speak that which is contrary to himself or to his own commands, as for instance:

When Christ began to teach to his disciples that the Son of Man must suffer many things and be rejected of the elders and chief priests and scribes, and be killed, and the third day rise, he spake that saying openly, and Peter took him and began to rebuke him, but he rebuked Peter, saying, "Get thee behind me Satan," from whence we may observe,

That whatsoever consequence or argument any man shall seem to enforce (though pretending Scripture for the same) that oppose themselves against duty, or do hinder the servants of God, therein I may say of such consequences, and such arguments, "Get thee behind me, Satan, thou art an offence to me." It is clear that Christ concludes those arguments and persuasions, whatsoever they be that do tend to the hinderance of any

---

[27] T.P.: The Covenant of Life not made to the seed of believers as coming out of their loins, & therefore the baptism of infants drawn by a false consequence.

solemn duty or ordinance of God, that they are of the devil, "Get thee behind me, Satan."

Therefore, all those books and arguments set out for the maintenance of children's baptism grounded upon this consequence, opposing themselves against duty, as you have heard, which is, that every penitent or believing person ought to be baptized.

Now the whole tendency of those books being to oppose the practice of the same, and to hinder it, I may say of them as Christ said before, &c. For upon this ground we may conclude all those discourses not to be of God, I shall therefore leave what is said to you seriously to weigh, whether or not this is an erroneous consequence.

But in the next place, let us come nearer to examine this consequence, both in itself, and the grounds from whence it is drawn.

The grounds of this consequence is that the Covenant of Grace belongs to believers' children. The consequence is therefore baptism, being an ordinance of that covenant, must needs belong to believers' children in which too lies our whole business. The grounds of this consequence is brought the Covenant of Circumcision, that belonging to Abraham and his seed after him in their generation (Gen. 17:17, 10–14).

From hence it is gathered that the Covenant of Grace, viz. of eternal life, belongs to believers and their seed born of their body. For the covenant God made to Abraham and his offspring, viz. the Covenant of Circumcision belonging to Abraham and his seed in their generation, therefore circumcision, the sign of the covenant, belong to them, so the New Covenant not belongs to believing Gentiles and their seed.

Baptism, being an ordinance of that covenant, belongs also to believing Gentiles, and their seed, this being the only and alone foundation ground of all those (except Papists) for their rantizing or sprinkling of children.

The Doctrine of Baptism

We shall endeavor to prove this ground (from whence this consequence flows) to be so far from being the truth that it is an error, and yea such an error, that if we were maintained with all those errors, that naturally must needs be defended as consequences of his opinion, it would shake the foundations of the Gospel. But that I may with much clear satisfaction inform others as God had clearly convinced my own soul of the truth of this, I shall propound this method to be handled.

First, then I shall make it appear to you that there [are] two covenants held forth in Scripture, the one a Covenant of Grace, and the other a Covenant of Works, or an absolute covenant, and a conditional covenant.

Secondly, I shall prove that the Covenant of Circumcision was no covenant of eternal life, but a conditional covenant, a Covenant of Works.

Thirdly, I shall prove that none but believers ever had, or shall have right to the Covenant of Grace.

Fourthly, I shall endeavor to answer such scriptures (especially those in the New Testament) that are usually alleged for defence of a covenant of life in the flesh.

5
Two Covenants, the One of Works, the Other of Grace, or the One Old, the Other New

To the first, that there [are] two covenants mentioned in Scripture, is very plain, the one a covenant of eternal life, the other a Covenant of Works, in which eternal life was not conveyed or given as appears in Jeremiah 31:31-34:

> But behold the day cometh, saith the Lord, that I will make a new covenant with the House of Israel, and with the House of Judah, not according to the Covenant that I made with their Fathers in the day that I took them by the hand to bring them out of the Land of Egypt, which my covenant they brake, although I was to them an husband saith the Lord.
> But this shall be the covenant that I will make with the house of Israel, after those days, saith the Lord; I will put my Law in their inward parts, and write it in their hearts, and will be their God, and they shall be my people, and they shall teach no more every man his neighbor, and every man his brother, saying, Know the Lord; for they shall all know me from the least of them unto the greatest of them, saith the Lord, for I will forgive their iniquities and remember their sins no more.

You have here set forth two covenants, the one Old, the other New, and as here we find a New and Old Covenant, so there is likewise, mention of two covenants in the eighth [chapter] to the Hebrews, where you have upon the matter the very same words, only it is clear, that Jesus Christ is the minister of the New Covenant in the 6th and 7th verses of that chap[ter]: "But now hath he obtained a more excellent ministry, by how much also he is the mediator of a better covenant, which was established upon better promises," for if that first

Covenant had been faultless, there would no place have been sought for the second.

In which place we may understand two covenants, a New Covenant and an Old Covenant (unto the Church then gathered all those that are in Christ, being God's Israel, Abraham's seed).

If you be in Christ then are ye Abraham's seed, and heirs according to the promise (Gal. 3), the latter end. So that those that are Christ's have this covenant now made to them, and it appears at the 3rd verse that the other covenant was a mere covenant of works in that he saith he hath made the first old.

And now that which waxeth old is ready to vanish away whereby the Old Covenant he means that typical Covenant of Works, which run upon the fleshly line of Abraham, and so put an end to that covenant in the flesh, and this you have further proved in Hebrews 9:15–16. There is again mention made of two Covenants or Testaments, the first and second, the first was confirmed by the blood of goats and calves, the second by the blood of Christ. Now if any please but to search the scriptures it will appear that there [are] two real distinct Covenants or Testaments, the one of grace, and the other of works, the one conditional, the other absolute. Now an absolute covenant is a covenant without all condition required in the creature, but what God himself performs as Jeremiah 32:40: "I will make an everlasting covenant with them, that I will not turn away from them to do them good, but I will put my fear in their hearts that they shall not depart from me," where you see God undertakes both. First, that he will not leave or forsake his people, but do them good; and secondly, undertakes that he will plant his fear in their hearts, that they shall depart from him.

And as in the eight[th] [chapter] of Hebrews, he engaged that he will write his law in their hearts, and that he will be their God, and they shall be his people, and that he will teach them to know him, and will pardon their iniquities, and their sins he will remember no more.

Now here is nothing but what God hath undertaken to perform, and to work in the creature as further appears in Ezekiel 16, latter end. "For thus saith the Lord God, I will even deal with thee as thou hast done, which hath despised the oath in breaking the covenant. Notwithstanding I will remember my covenant with thee in the day of thy youth, and I will establish unto thee an everlasting covenant," and as he saith afterward, "not by thy covenant, but by my covenant," so that which he calls "thy covenant" was that which they broke, and therein despised the oath as he saith plainly, holding forth that it was a covenant of works answerable to that in Nehemiah 10:29: "They clave to their brethren the nobles, and entered into a curse and an oath to walk in God's law which was given by Moses the servant of God."

In which case you may discern here was two covenants, the one that God calls his covenant, and another, that was their covenant, a covenant of works which they broke. And likewise you have further the covenant of eternal life opened in Ezekiel 36:25–27:

> Then will I sprinkle clean water upon you, and you shall be clean from all your filthiness, and from your idols will I cleanse you. A new heart also will I give you, and a new Spirit will I put within you, and I will take away the stony heart out of your flesh, and will give you a heart of flesh, and I will put my Spirit within you, and cause you to walk in my statutes, and you shall keep my judgments and do them.

Where you have, as I said before, this New Covenant wholly lying on God's part, that he would first cleanse them from all their idols, and iniquities, that he undertakes to give a new heart, to take away the heart of stone, and to give them hearts of flesh. And that he will give the soul his own Spirit, and thereby came these to walk in his ways whom he calls to the obedience of his truth.

If they sin, he binds himself to pardon their sins, and to remember their sins and transgressions no more, so that it is impossible that this covenant should be broke[en], or that a soul shall ever miscarry, that is once in this covenant, as in respect of his everlasting estate. And to this purpose, David very eminently speaks in 2 Samuel 23 and verse 5, "Although my house be not so with God, yet he hath made with me an everlasting covenant, ordered in all things and sure, for this is all my salvation, and all my desire, although he make it not to grow," where you have David setting out the Covenant of Grace, and the mercies in it to be in all points perfect and sure.

And to this purpose the Prophet in the 55[th chapter] of Isaiah, and the third verse, inviting souls and persuading them to come to Christ, saith, "Incline your ear, and come unto me. Hear and your souls shall live, and I will make an everlasting covenant with you, even the sure mercies of David." That is, he will give a soul those covenant mercies which are most sure, no way depending upon any condition to be performed in the creature, but wholly upon the Lord, as appears in Psalm 89, 28th to the 37th verse:

> My mercy will I keep for him forevermore, and my covenant shall stand fast with him; his seed also will I make to endure forever, and his throne as the days of Heaven. If his children forsake my law, and walk not in my judgments, if they break, and keep not my commandments, then will I visit their transgressions with the rod, and their iniquities with stripes. Nevertheless my loving kindness will I not entirely take from him, nor suffer my faithfulness to fail. My covenant will I not break, nor alter the thing which is gone out of my lips. Once have I sworn by my holiness that I will not lie unto David. His seed shall endure forever, his throne as the sun before me, it shall

The Doctrine of Baptism

be established forever, as the moon, and as a faithful witness in Heaven, Selah.

Now in these words you have the Covenant of Eternal Life made with Christ and his spiritual seed whom David and his seed were types of, which covenant is a sure covenant to all those to whom it is once made, and to this doth the author of Hebrews alludes, when he saith in 6:17-18:

> Wherein God willing more abundantly to shew unto the heirs of promise the immutability of his counsel, confirmed by an oath, that by two immutable things in which it was impossible for God to lie, we might have strong consolation, who have fled for refuge to lay hold upon the hope set before us.

Now in this covenant before spoken to, you have both the promise and oath here spoken of, and here in this covenant must needs be discovered, the immutability of his counsel because this is as David saith, "a covenant that is in all points perfect and sure,"[28] and James, in his epistle, alluding to these New Covenant blessings, or gifts, saith, "Every good and perfect gift is from above, and cometh down from the Father of lights, with whom there is no variableness, nor shadow of turning,"[29] and that he doth here speak of the New Covenant gifts doth appear in the next words he saith, "Of his own will begat he us with the word of truth, that we should be a kind of first fruits of his creatures."[30]

Now consider well that in this covenant there is nothing that he requires, but he engageth himself to enable us to accomplish. If he commands to pray, he promises to give his Spirit to help our infirmities. If he commands to walk in all his ways, as you

---

[28] 2 Samuel 23:5.
[29] James 1:17.
[30] James 1:18.

have heard, he promiseth that he will put his Spirit in them to cause them to walk in his ways.

Why though the Covenant of Grace be absolute, yet the promises are held forth under a condition

But some may object and say, That we find the Gospel is held out upon condition of faith and repentance.

Answer. It is true, the promise of salvation and remission of sins is held out with a condition to the world because it is God's free mercy to work that condition in the hearts of his elect, by means of preaching and tendering of the Gospel, and in them only.

But we are not to think that this grace of faith and repentance are any qualifications that persons are to attain by their own abilities unto which the Gospel is tendered.

But in the New Covenant, the Lord undertakes to work the condition, and to give the salvation tendered upon that condition also, for saith he, "I will be unto you a God, and you shall be unto me a people;" and in particular he saith, He "will put his law in their hearts, and in their minds will he write them, and he will teach them to know him."

Now doubtless the law of faith and repentance are here included according to those scriptures: "For by grace are you saved through faith, and that not of yourselves. It is the gift of God" (Eph. 2:8).

Faith the gift of God

Where he holds forth that though faith be as [an] instrumental means of our salvation, yet it is God's free gift wrought in us, [and] therefore surely a covenant gift. Paul upon this ground in Philippians 1:28 saith, "It is not only given us to believe, but to suffer for his name's sake, where to believe, it is given of God," and so in Acts 18:27, speaking of Apollos, saith, that when he came, he helped them much who had believed through grace, as in Hebrews 12:2, where Jesus is said to be as well the author as the finisher of our faith.

All which passages do show that faith is as well given in the New Covenant as the salvation tendered upon that condition.

Repentance the gift of God
And so is also repentance a New Covenant gift as well as remission of sins tendered upon that condition, as you find in Acts 5:31: "Him hath God exalted with his own right hand to be a prince and savior, to give repentance to Israel, and remission of sins;" and in Acts 11:18: "When they heard those things they held their peace and glorified God, saying, then hath God also to the Gentiles granted repentance unto life."

Where observe, to God's Israel, both of Jews and Gentiles, God doth grant and freely give repentance as well as salvation and remission of sins, promised upon condition of repentance. This likewise appears in 2 Timothy 2:25, where the ministers of God are commanded in meekness to instruct those that oppose themselves, if God peradventure will at any time give them repentance to the acknowledging of the truth. This doth plainly prove that though repentance and faith be the condition that the Gospel is tendered on, yet you see the Lord doth in the New Covenant give faith and repentance as well as remission of sins, and eternal life.

The Covenant of Grace obscurely delivered to our first parents
And further I shall make appear that this Covenant of Grace to eternal life was first more obscurely and darkly revealed to our first parents. God directing his speech to the devil in Genesis 3:16[31] for the greater terror of the devil and the greater comfort of his Elect, God saith, "I will put enmity between thy seed and the seed of the woman; it shall bruise thy head, and thou shalt bruise his heal."

---

[31]Actually, Genesis 3:15.

The speech in substance contains the Covenant of Grace, Christ the true spiritual seed being here promised, who in Scripture is held forth to be the very substance and marrow of the New Covenant. Therefore the Lord saith in Isaiah 42:6, speaking of Christ, "I will give thee a Covenant of the people, a light to the Gentiles," where the very gift of Christ is called a covenant because where he is promised, all heavenly and spiritual blessings are there given, all the promises being in Christ, Yea, and in him, Amen (2 Cor. 1:20). And all spiritual and heavenly blessings are in him (Eph. 1:3), he saith [that] he will put enmity between the seed of the serpent and the seed of the woman, which must needs have thus much in it.

That God would put or infuse in the seed of the woman his created gifts of holiness and purity, and the precious love of God, whereupon must needs be, that this new nature would be hated by the Devil as being opposite to him, and also must needs hate the Devil with his evil nature as the Psalmist saith, "Ye that love God, hate evil."[32] Christ tell us in Matthew 10:34:

> Think not that I come to send peace on the earth; I come not to send peace, but a sword; for I am come to set a man at variance against his father, and his daughter against her mother, and the daughter-in-law against the mother-in-law, and a man's foes shall be they of his own household.

And Luke saith, five in one house shall be divided, three against two, and two against three (Luke 12:52). And what should occasion this division but that new nature which the Lord infuseth into his own seed or children, which cannot comply with the seed of the Serpent? So Peter saith, "They spake evil of us because we run not with them to the same excess of riot" (1 Pet. 4:4).

---

[32] Psalm 97:10.

So that I understand that here in this third of Genesis is the whole New Covenant included.

The New Covenant not entailed upon any fleshly line

This New Covenant was never entailed upon any fleshly line or generation as the covenant of circumcision was, but was still confirmed of God in Christ, and to such souls only in Christ as you find in the promise to Abraham: "In thee shall all the nations of the earth be blessed" (Gen. 12:3).

Where you may observe, that here is no respect of persons in the matter of these blessings to everlasting life, but all nations in Christ as well as one nation as another, if in Christ, have those blessings promised to them, and thus much is employed in that promise that all nations out of him are accursed.

What is the blessedness promised to Abraham and his seed?
But God here directs his speech to Abraham (some may say) it is true, but with respect to Christ now who, as touching the flesh, was in his loins, and this blessedness or justification of life, which was confirmed in Abraham as a father of all nations, is by the Apostle Paul called the Gospel, "The Scripture, foreseeing that God would justify the heathen through faith, preached the Gospel to Abraham, as it is written, "In thee shall all the nations of the earth be blessed" (Gal. 3:8). So this blessedness spoken of in Genesis 12:3 is expounded by Paul to be justification by faith in Christ, and in Acts 3 this blessedness is there expounded to be a turning of every one of them from their iniquities (Acts 3:26).

And also this Gospel promise or covenant is spoken to in Genesis 15:5 where he bids Abraham look up to the heavens, and if he could number the stars of heaven, and the sands upon the seashore, so shall his seed be. Abraham believed God, and it was accounted him for righteousness. This promise is quoted by the Apostle Paul as the Gospel Covenant in Romans 4:3 in opposition to the covenant of circumcision entailed upon the flesh or fleshly line of Abraham. For circumcision was a covenant in the flesh, as the apostle calls it, which he also expounds in the 1st and 2nd v[erse] to be a covenant of works. But more of that hereafter, only that which I would observe at present is that the apostle confirms that the Gospel promise in Genesis 12 and verse 3 and Genesis 15 and ver[se] 5 to be the New Covenant, wherein was given, through faith, the justification of life, excluding in this point the Covenant of Circumcision, called works; both these covenants are made with Abraham in Genesis 17 (see Rom. 4:1-2). There you find the New Covenant made with him to the 6th verse and from the 7th verse to the 14th the covenant of circumcision in the flesh. The New Covenant is expressed in the third verse where he saith, "As for me my covenant shall be with thee, and thou shalt be a father to many nations, or of a multitude of nations, and thy name shall be no more called Abram, but Abraham, for a father of a multitude of nations have I made thee." This is by the Apostle Paul in Romans 4:17-18 held out to be the Covenant of Life, which he doth clearly hold distinct and different from the Covenant of Circumcision in that place, denying that Abraham or his spiritual seed had their justification in the Covenant of Circumcision, but bringing in this that Abraham should be a father of many nations, and so shall thy seed be, as that in which Abraham and his spiritual seed, whether Jews or Gentiles, were and should be justified.

And this promise or covenant is made with Abraham in Genesis 18:18: "In thee shall all the nations of the earth be blessed." So long as Christ was according to the flesh in Abraham's loins, the promise runs thus: "In thee," meaning that through Christ, which then was in him, should all nations of the earth be blessed.

But as soon as Isaac was come out of Abraham's loins, as in Genesis 22:18, then, saith he, "In thy seed shall all the nations of the earth be blessed," whereby "seed" most strictly is to be understood [as] Christ as the Apostle Paul intimates in Gal. 3:16 where he expounds this word, "seed," to be not "seeds" as of many, but "seed" as of one, which is Christ. So this blessedness in the seed, Christ, is here expounded to be God's confirming his covenant in Christ, and note that this blessedness, which David holds out to be the covenant confirmed of God in Christ, it was not entailed upon the flesh of Abraham and his fleshly seed, but made in Abraham as a father of all the spiritual seed in all nations, and confirmed in the seed of Christ to all nations.

Here the Jews, after the flesh, have no more interest than any other nation, except it be by faith, for faith only unites to this seed, and gives an in-being in the same.

This blessedness is expounded by David in Psalm 32, [the] last ver[se], to lie in remission of sins, and purgation of the heart from guile, and expounded by the apostle in Acts 3, the last ver[se] to be a turning everyone from his iniquities. For so there, Peter expounds this blessedness confirmed in Abraham and his seed. And though Christ did fulfill this covenant to the elect of the Jews, yet the rest were hardened, and were never in this sense blessed, either in the point of justification or purgation from sin, because they were never in Christ, the true seed by faith, nor never were thereby the spiritual seed of Abraham, walking in the steps of his faith, as all his spiritual seed did, Romans 4:12 and Galatians 3:29: "If you be in Christ, then you are Abraham's seed, and heirs according to the promise."

Thus I have given you from clear light of Scripture that there were two covenants, a Covenant of Grace, and a Covenant of Works; the Covenant of Grace belonging to Abraham, and his spiritual seed in Christ, and all along from Adam, to all the spiritual seed of the woman, that were born of promise as the apostle describes the spiritual seed in Romans 9:8, for he saith such are accounted the seed that are so born of promise. And so at this day all nations, both Jews and Gentiles that are born again, they are the seed and children that only have an interest in the promise of salvation. And so much for the first head.

6
Circumcision Proved to Be No Covenant of Eternal Life, but a Typical and Carnal Covenant

Now I come to the next place to prove, that the Covenant of Circumcision is no covenant of eternal life, but a typical covenant, yea a Covenant of Works, which is also called by the Lord a covenant of flesh (Gen. 17:13), and therefore to be sure no covenant of eternal life.

But for the better clearing of the truth of this I shall first expound some words in the covenant, that is the word "everlasting covenant." That word seems to some to hold forth a Covenant of Life because it is said to be everlasting, whereas the word, "everlasting," used in this covenant, is to be understood only for the ever of the Law for the time of the Jewish state as always the word is to be understood when applied to the Jews of their generation. As for example, in the 16th [chapter] of Leviticus it is said the [High] Priest should make atonement for the holy sanctuary, an atonement for the tabernacle of the congregation, and for the altar, and shall he make an atonement for the priests, and for all the people of the congregation, and this shall be an everlasting statute to you to make an atonement for the children of Israel for all their sins once a year. This "everlasting" here must needs be understood but till Christ came. And so in Numbers 25:13: "He shall have it, and his seed after him, even the covenant of an everlasting priesthood, because he was zealous for his God, and made an atonement for the children of Israel," speaking here only of a ceremonial priesthood, typing out Jesus Christ, the substance that was to put an end to it.

How the word "everlasting" is taken in the Law

And so this Covenant of Circumcision is to be understood as everlasting as Canaan, and the possession thereof, which was until Christ's coming who was the substance thereof, this being a maxim: that whatsoever the word, "everlasting," or ever hath this joined with it, to you, or to your seed in their generation, that then it is to be understood only for the ever of the Law, and the time period of that ministration till Christ come, and no longer, Exodus 40:15: "Thou shalt anoint them as thou didst anoint their fathers, that they may minister unto me in the priests' offices; for their anointing shall surely be an everlasting priesthood throughout their generations." And so you have it in Exodus 30:20–21: Moses saying, "When they go into the tabernacle of the congregation, they shall wash with water that they die not; and when they come near the altar to minister, to burn offerings made by fire unto the Lord, so they shall wash their hands and their feet that they die not; and it shall be a statute forever to them, even to him, and his seed throughout their generations."

The next word that I would like to speak to is "I will be to thee a God, and thy seed after thee," which to some seems to hold forth a Covenant of Grace in that he gives himself as a God in this covenant.

To which I answer, that God either gives and makes himself over in a Covenant of Works, which is upon a condition of works done in the creature, or else he gives himself in an absolute Covenant of Grace in Christ Jesus the Mediator without all the condition of works to be fulfilled in the creature.

First argument to prove circumcision a Covenant of Works

I shall make it clear, that God no otherwise gives himself in the Covenant of Circumcision but conditionally, which is the first argument that I shall use to prove the Covenant of Circumcision to be a Covenant of Works [and] not a Covenant of Eternal Life because it is conditional, what God promiseth to be or give to Abraham and his fleshly seed in their generations; it was upon a condition that Abraham and his seed should keep his covenant on their parts as clearly appears (Gen. 17:7-8 to verse 14), where you find the Lord engageth himself to Abraham, and his fleshly seed to be their God and to give them the whole land of Canaan. In that sense he would be their God, to possess them of that good land, and all the blessings of the same, upon condition that they should keep his covenant on their part, both he and his generation after him.

And the subject matter of the covenant that they should keep is that he should be circumcised, and circumcise all born in his house and bought with money. But though circumcision only be here mentioned, yet all the works of the Law at that time made known to Abraham, are there included, as the apostle expounds it, who best understood that Scripture, Romans 2:25: "For circumcision verily profiteth if thou keep the Law, but if thou be a breaker of the Law, thy circumcision shall be made uncircumcision." And so you have it in Galatians 5:1-3: "Stand fast," saith the apostle, "in the liberty where Christ hath made you free, and be not entangled again with the yoke of bondage," which in Acts 15 it is said, "Neither they, nor their fathers, were able to bear." But verse 2: "Behold, I Paul say unto you, that if you be circumcised, Christ shall profit you nothing, for I testify again to every man that is circumcised, that he is a debtor to do the whole Law." And so much is clearly held forth in Galatians 6:12-13, where saith the apostle, "As many as desire to make a fair show in the flesh, they constrain you to be circumcised, only least they should suffer persecution for the cross of Christ; for neither they themselves who are circumcised, keep the Law, but desire you to be circumcised that they may glory in your flesh."

Where you may observe, that for men to be circumcised themselves, and not to keep the law, or otherwise to press it upon others, the apostles hold it to be absurd if withal they did not keep the Law that were thus circumcised.

And in the text before quoted, it is clear that circumcision (in the nature of it) binds them ever to keep the Law. And to this purpose you find in Acts 15: "There were certain teachers that taught the brethren, That except they were circumcised, they could not be saved," upon which the apostles come together, and in the 10th verse Peter saith, "Why tempt you God to lay a yoke upon the disciples' necks, which neither our Fathers, nor we are able to bear?" And what was this yoke, but that they were to be circumcised and to keep the Law?

So that circumcision was that which did comprehend under it the Covenant of Works, or the yoke of bondage that Paul in Galatians 5:1-3 bids Christians stand fast in their liberty or freedom from that covenant or yoke of bondage which Jesus Christ had freed them from.

So that you may see that all the observation of the Law, which we are set at liberty from by Christ Jesus his death, was included in the Law of Circumcision. So that in effect, here you have the covenants: Abraham (as if God should say), I will be a God to thee, and to thy seed after thee in their generations, to protect, defend, and deliver thee, to bless thee, and the fruit of thy womb, in the basket, and in their store, in all their outward blessings, upon condition that thou and they will be circumcised and keep the Law. Thus God makes a covenant upon condition so that if they fail on their part, then he is left at liberty to fail on his part, as that notable expression in Jeremiah 11:2-5,

> Hear the word of the Covenant, and speak unto the men of Judah, to the inhabitants of Jerusalem, and say thou unto them, Thus saith the Lord God of Israel, Cursed be the man that obeyeth not the words of this Covenant, which I commanded unto your Father when I brought them from the Land of Egypt, from the iron furnace, saying, Obey my voice and do according to all these things

which I command you so shall ye be my people, and I will be your God, that I might confirm the oath that I have sworn unto your fathers, to give them a land which floweth with milk and honey as appeareth this day.

Whence you may clearly observe, that God gives himself to be their God, and the blessing of Canaan upon condition that they would keep the Law, "so shall ye be my people, and I will be your God."

Now you must mind, Abraham had a new covenant of life made with him when he was 75 years old (Gen. 12:4), which was 24 years before this time, that he had the Covenant of Circumcision, and his happiness with all his spiritual seed, was and is in that absolute covenant, confirmed by God in Christ, which stands in force still to believers in all nations. But this Covenant of Circumcision was conditional, and not absolute, therefore not a Covenant of Life, but a Covenant of Works.

Second argument to prove circumcision a Covenant of Works

The second ground why the Covenant of Circumcision must needs be a Covenant of Works, a typical covenant, a covenant in the flesh, as in Genesis 17:13: "He that is born in thy house, and he that is bought without money, must needs be circumcised, so my covenant shall be in your flesh for an everlasting covenant." To be sure such is not the Covenant of Grace to eternal life, for that was confirmed of God in Christ, as you hear, to all nations. "In thee shall all the nations of the earth be blessed" (Gen. 12:3), and "in thy seed shall all the nations of the earth be blessed" (Gen. 22:18), as I have formerly spoken to.

But the Lord saith of this Covenant of Circumcision that it shall be in their flesh for an everlasting covenant. It is manifested by the Apostle Paul, that this is therefore a Covenant of Works (Rom. 4:1-2), saith he, "What shall we say then, that

Abraham our father as appertaining to the flesh hath found? For if Abraham was justified by works, he hath whereof to glory, but not before God."

These words are inferred by the Apostle Paul for the prevention of an objection that might justly be in the mind of the Romans occasioned by the apostle's former answer. For though the apostle had granted in the beginning of the third chapter, that the circumcised Jews, were in some respect privileged above other nations, and that chiefly, in those eminent tenders and offers that the Gospel held out amongst them, which though it proved not effectual to all, yet [to] the minds of some it was effectual. But yet after in verse 9, the apostle begins to manifest his understanding that to be a Jew after the flesh, and to be in the Covenant of Circumcision, did not free men from the guilt of damnation no more than other men that were heathens that were not Jews after the flesh, neither circumcised.

To this purpose he states a question, "What then? Are we better than they? No, in no wise. For we have before proved, that both Jew and Gentile, are all under sin, as it is written, 'there is non[e] righteous, no not one'." The apostle goes on to prove, "That the Jews after the flesh (in the Covenant of Circumcision) were equally in a damnable and sinful condition with the poor heathenish infidels, all equally guilty before God, verse 19. And his inference is in verse 20, "That therefore by the works of the Law no flesh should be justified in his sight," clearly holding forth, that to be a Jew, and circumcised, and to be under the Law, is the selfsame thing. And when the apostle had concluded that being a Jew, in the Covenant of Circumcision, did in no way difference him from the heathen, as to life, he now shows what way both Jews and Gentiles come to the justification of life, and that is freely by God's grace through the redemption that is in Christ Jesus whom God hath set forth to be a propitiation through faith in his blood. Therefore he excludes the Law of Works, wholly in the matter of justification,

The Doctrine of Baptism

and brings in the Law of Faith, showing clearly that he hath put one way to justify both Jew and Gentile, which is by faith in Jesus Christ, the true promised seed in the new covenant.

Upon these words the Romans seemed thus to argue [in] chap. 4, verse 1, Is it so, that a man may be a Jew, and have interest in the Covenant of Circumcision entailed upon the fleshly line, and seed of Abraham, and yet be not better than pagans or heathens as to the matter of life? "What shall we then say, that Abraham our father, as appertaining to the flesh, hath found?" As if they should say: "if a man may be a Jew of the seed of Abraham, and so of the Covenant of Circumcision, and as to the matter of justification and eternal life, be nearer than a profane Gentile that is not Abraham's seed, nor hath any interest in the covenant?" What privilege doth Abraham hath in the covenant appertaining to, or entailed on the flesh?"

Unto which the apostle answers in the second and third verses, and so along in [the 4th chapter] of the Romans, clearly distinguishing two covenants, the one of circumcision, a covenant of works, the other, a promise of Jesus Christ, and made to the faith of such as believe. Therefore saith the apostle in [the] [2nd verse], and so forward: "If Abraham were justified by works, he hath whereof to glory, but not before God," plainly interpreting that the covenant with our father Abraham had interest in, as appertaining to the flesh of him and his seed after him in their generations, was a Covenant of Works in which Abraham had nothing to glory before God, the reason is given because he was justified before God in another covenant or promise [in] Genesis 15:5-6: "For what saith the Scripture? Abraham believed God, and it was accompted[33] to him for righteousness."

And thus the apostle goes along, showing that justification was not to be had in the Covenant of Works entailed on the flesh of Abraham, but by faith in the Covenant of Grace, the promised

---

[33] Accounted.

seed, which he proves by David's testimony in Psalm 32:1-2, set down in 6th, 7th, and [8th] verses of this chapter.

Now thus much being said, he states the question, whether this grace of justification "came upon the circumcision only, or the uncircumcision also? For we say, that faith was reckoned unto Abraham for righteousness."

Now here is the question, seeing that Abraham had two covenants made with him, one the Gospel of Faith, and the other, a covenant in the flesh, in which of these had he his justification to eternal life?

The answer is plain, for saith the apostle, not in circumcision, he was not justified in or by the Covenant of Circumcision, but in the promise of the promised seed which God is said to give [as] a covenant for his people by faith in that seed; even in uncircumcision was Abraham justified, and that (as I said before) 24 years before the Covenant of Circumcision was made with him, he was justified, believing in the promise of the Messiah that was to come out of his loins, according to the flesh, "in whom all the nations of the earth should be blessed."

Now God, promising that the Messiah, according to the flesh, should come out of Abraham, viz. out of his loins or his flesh, and this was then a great article of his faith, that he was to believe to righteousness not only that justification was to be had, and blessedness to be had, but it must be had in that seed that was to come out of Abraham according to the flesh.

And as a confirmation and seal of this public righteousness, confirmed in Abraham in an external covenant, to point out to all the world that as verily as God did take this nation (according to the flesh) to himself by this external covenant, so would God be incarnate in this flesh.

And as the flesh of the foreskin of the member of generation must be cut or bruised, and blood shed by which a Jew, according to the flesh, was bound to keep the Law, this I understand did figure out, how Christ, the true seed of Abraham, descending out of his loins by generation, should (considered as male and not female) by breaking his flesh, and shedding his blood, fulfill and satisfy the Law.

So that this covenant of circumcision was of sealing use to Abraham to confirm this other covenant, and a school master to lead to Christ, as all other branches of the Old Covenant were. Therefore, saith Paul in Romans 4:11: "Moreover he received the sign of circumcision, a seal of the righteousness of faith, which he had, being uncircumcised, that he might be the father of all that believe."

The sealing use of circumcision
proved to be peculiar unto Abraham
Where observe, the apostle calls not circumcision a seal, but a sign, "He received the sign of circumcision, a seal of the righteousness of faith which he had being uncircumcised." There are these reasons in the text that restrain the sealing use of circumcision only to Abraham.

First, because this righteousness of faith, the text saith that he had before he was circumcised. Therefore, good reason might be sealed or confirmed, having it before he received the sign of circumcision, a seal of the righteousness of faith which he had being uncircumcised. But his posterity after him, at eight days old cannot be said that they had this righteousness of faith to seal, having it not preceding their circumcision.

The second reason the text affords us is that he might be the father of all that believe. This is the main reason the apostle insists upon: "He received the sign of circumcision, a seal of the righteousness of faith, that he might be the father of all who believe."

This reason cannot be [applied] to any of Abraham's posterity besides himself, for they were not the fathers of all who believe. That was proper to Abraham to be a high father, or a father of all nations; therefore, as I said before, God promising in

Abraham that public righteousness as a father of all nations in the Covenant of Grace adds to the covenant and external covenant to be entailed in his line and in his flesh as confirmation of the same.

A third reason is this. Here is the Spirit of God affirming the sealing use of circumcision to Abraham only, and not to any one of his fleshly seed, and as before, upon a reason special to Abraham. Now where the Scripture hath not a mouth to speak, we must not have an ear to hear. But the Scripture here only affirms circumcision to be a seal of the righteousness of faith to Abraham, and affords no such thing as to his seed.

A fourth reason lies in verse 13: That the promise to Abraham "to be the heir of the world was not to him, nor his seed through the Law, that is, through the Covenant of Circumcision, but through the righteousness of faith."

"For if they which are of the Law be heirs, then faith is made void, and the promises of none effect." Because the Law worketh wrath." "Therefore, it is of faith, that it might be by grace to the end the promises might be sure to all the seed. Not to that only which is of the Law, but to that also which is of the faith of Abraham who is the father of us all, as it is written, "I have made thee a father of many nations, before him who believed, even God, who quickeneth the dead."[34]

So that there is not in all the Scripture a place more clearly [that] proves the Covenant of Circumcision entailed on the fleshly line of Abraham to be a Covenant of Works than this 4[th chapter] of the Romans, clearing and setting the Covenant of Circumcision and faith in opposition, holding forth that Abraham, and all his spiritual seed, had their justification in another covenant, and not in the Covenant of Circumcision, clearly holding forth the Covenant of Circumcision to be works and not grace, which doth sufficiently prove that the Covenant of Circumcision had no promise of justification or eternal life in it.

---

[34] Romans 4:14–17.

The Doctrine of Baptism

An appendix to the second argument to prove circumcision a Covenant of Works

But further, that the covenant entailed on the flesh must needs be understood a covenant of works, viz. that of circumcision appears in Philippians 3:2-4, and so forward, where saith the apostle, "Beware of dogs, beware of evil workers, beware of the concision; for we are the circumcision that worship God in the Spirit, and rejoice in Jesus Christ, and put no confidence in the flesh." By "flesh" he means the covenant entailed upon the flesh, the Covenant of Circumcision. It is plain by this answer, for he saith, "if any man thinketh he hath whereof to trust in the flesh, I more, circumcised the eighth day, the stock of Israel, of the tribe of Benjamin, a Hebrew of the Hebrews, as touching the Law, a Pharisee, concerning zeal, persecuting the Church, touching the righteousness of the Law, blameless."

And this he sets by no more than dung or dross in comparison of the other covenant or promise of Christ, righteousness, and salvation by him which he received by faith, and he suffered the loss of all things for the sake of him, and did accompt[35] all the whole privilege of circumcision, and the Covenant of Works, to be but as dung that he might win Christ. So if this promise of salvation and justification by him, had been given in the covenant of the flesh, and line of Abraham, then it had been very improper for Paul to accompt this as dung, and to cast contempt upon it, as that which was wholly void of Christ. It would be very sinful for any man in such a case to cast such contempt upon the Covenant of Grace itself and the privileges thereof peculiarly relating to the same.

But you see, Paul doth clearly distinguish two covenants, the one of faith, the other of circumcision. This will further appear in Galatians 3:3: "Are ye so foolish that having begun in the Spirit, are ye now made perfect in the flesh?" Where he again distinguisheth two covenants, the one spiritual, the other a

---

[35] Account.

fleshly covenant. The Galatians, having at the first hearing of him, begun to embrace the Gospel or the Spirit or spiritual word of the New Covenant, and now they would join the Covenant of Works in the flesh with the Gospel, which, it is evident, he means the Covenant of Circumcision, which here they would seek to be perfected by.

Therefore in Galatians 4, [the] latter end, he clearly distinguisheth between two covenants under the figure of Sarah and Hagar, and two seeds, holding forth the Covenant of Circumcision to be the Covenant of Works, and to be that bondwoman (as it were) in chap[ter] 5:1-3 [and] chap[ter] 6:12-13. So that if you will seriously mind these scriptures, they do most evidently prove that the Covenant of Circumcision, made in the flesh or fleshly line of Abraham, is a Covenant of Works, and that which the Gospel or Covenant of Grace, is set in opposition to; and as this covenant of circumcision is set in opposition to the Covenant of Eternal life as having all the works of the Law included in it, so consider the New Covenant speaks thus, "I will lay my Law in your hearts, and in your minds will I write them."[36] But circumcision is a covenant not in the heart, but in the flesh only as you have heard. This is the second ground why the Covenant of Circumcision cannot be a covenant of eternal life, but a covenant of works only.

Third argument to prove circumcision a Covenant of Works
The third reason to prove circumcision to be a Covenant of Works, and not of eternal life is because that there is no promise of eternal life in it, but of temporal blessings in the land of Canaan, and that God promising himself to be a God, is only in that respect, as to outward protection and provision in the land of Canaan, and other like privileges. And that is noted by the apostle in Hebrews 8:6: "But now hath he obtained a more excellent

---

[36] Hebrews 10:16.

ministry, by how much also he is a mediator of a better covenant which was established upon better promises."

Herein he clearly doth show that the covenant, waxing old and vanishing away, was grounded upon worse promises, which must needs be understood [as] temporal promises, as in Jeremiah 11:25:

> Hear ye the words of this covenant, and speak unto the men of Judah, and the inhabitants of Jerusalem, and say unto them, "Thus saith the Lord God of Israel, Cursed be the man that obeyeth not the words of this covenant, which I commanded your Fathers in the day that brought them out of the land of Egypt, from the iron furnace, saying, 'Obey my voice and do them, according to all which I command you.' So shall ye be my people, and I will be your God, that I may perform the oath that I have sworn unto your fathers, to give them a land flowing with milk and honey, as it is this day;" then answered I and said, "So be it Lord."

Where you have this covenant of God's being his people's God, and giving them Canaan, annexed to the works of the Law as being all one covenant.

Observe the words in the text, "So shall ye be my people, and I will be your God, that I may perform the covenant which I have sworn to your fathers to give them a land flowing with milk and honey."

You shall see the promises of Canaan, the blessings thereof, are annexed to the Law of works, Deuteronomy 30:15:

> See, I have set before thee life and good, and death and evil, in that I command thee this day, to love the Lord thy God, to walk in his ways, and to keep his commandments, and statutes, and his judgments, that thou mayst live and multiply, and the Lord thy God shall bless thee in the land whither thou goest to possess it.

And so in the last verse, where he presseth the people to obey his voice, that they might dwell in in the land that the Lord swear unto their fathers, to Abraham, Isaac, and Jacob to give them. And so in Deuteronomy 7:12-13:

> Wherefore it shall come to pass that if you hearken to those judgments to keep and do them, that then the Lord shall keep unto thee the covenant and the mercy that he swore to thy fathers; and he will love thee and bless, and multiply thee, he will also bless thee; he will also bless thee in the fruit of thy womb, and the fruit of thy land, thy corn, and thy wine, and thine oil, the increase of thy kine[37] and the flock of thy sheep in the land which he swore unto thy fathers before thee.

So that you see, the Covenant of God, giving himself a God to the national people of the Jews, in relation to the blessing of Canaan, was still upon obedience to the works of the Law; that this covenant which God elected to himself the body of Israel, in, and by which he separated them to himself from all the nations of the earth, it is clear was a Covenant of Works, wherein the people were bound to outward observance, and worship, and service to God. Upon this condition would God be their God, and give them Canaan. For there is a vast difference in God's making over himself to be a God to a people in a conditional covenant of works out of Christ, and an absolute covenant established of God in Christ. For in such a covenant he was never the God of the whole family of Abraham, or Church of Israel. "The elect obtained that, the rest were hardened," as in Romans 11:17.

Fourth argument to prove circumcision a Covenant of Works
The fourth ground is this, that a man, by laying out a little money, might have brought a person in this covenant, and

---
[37] Cattle.

THE DOCTRINE OF BAPTISM

interested him thereby into all the privileges of the same, which if this were a Covenant of Life, wherein the Spirit and spiritual gifts of the Lord had been given, a man might say as Peter did say to Simon Magus, "Thy money perish with thee."[38]

But for that reason, most certain it is that this Covenant of Circumcision is no spiritual covenant, which will appear in the words of the covenant in Genesis 17:12-13:

> And he that is eight days old shall be circumcised among you, every man child in your generations, he that is born in the house or bought with money of any stranger, which is not of thy seed. He that is born in thy house, and he that is bought with thy money must needs be circumcised, and my covenant shall be in your flesh for an everlasting covenant.

Where observe, that all bought with money must be circumcised so that if an Israelite should buy a black Moor, or the most savage heathen in the world, he was bound to see him circumcised, and being circumcised, he was now in the covenant. The truth is circumcision was one of those carnal ordinances that the author of Hebrews doth speak of that was appointed till the time of Reformation (Heb. 9:9).

Now the person which the Lord would have circumcised must be of the family of Abraham, and that is all the qualifications required: For God doth not require a person, so and so spiritually qualified, as he doth now under the Gospel. The Lord gives in general a law and commandment unto Abraham that all his family must be circumcised, and that he must see it performed.

It is not in the institution enjoined that the person that doth circumcise must be a believer, neither is it enjoined that the person upon whom it is done must have discipleship, or the work of grace, but this only, he must be one of the family of Abraham,

---

[38] Acts 8:20.

either born in his house, or bought with his money. And so the slave bought with money was as truly interested into the Covenant of God, and the right of eating the Passover as one born in the house of the seed of Abraham.

Fifth argument to prove circumcision a Covenant of Works
A fifth ground is this, that men (out of this covenant) might be saved, and such were really interested in it might be damned.

As for example, Lot dwelling in the city of Sodom, and all the godly that day in the whole world, excepting Abraham and his house, or family, were no way interessed in the Covenant of Circumcision, yet were saved, And Israel, who, or the multitude of them, were as the sand on the sea shore, and interessed in this covenant, yet but a remnant of them were saved (as Isa. 10:23). Lot is commended to be a just and righteous man, and yet this covenant was never made to him, nor his seed and posterity, the Ammonites and Moabites, which were as truly the seed and children of a believer as the seed of Abraham were. So you find Job in the land of Uz, in the Book of Job, and his four friends, and besides those of Job's friends, one of his friends doth intimate several other ancient and godly persons in those times, as [in] Job 8:8, 10, Job 15:10. For saith he, "Ask the ancients and they will tell thee, for we have those with us, much more elder than thy Father," which doth argue that there were very ancient, godly men fit to be inquired of, as touching those heavenly mysteries, that were much older than Job's father in the east country. And it is plain that neither they, nor any of their children or families, had right to circumcision, and the blessing of Canaan, but most sure it is they had interest in the Covenant of Life, which plainly shews that circumcision was but and earthly, typical covenant, such as good and godly men might not have interest in, and such as wicked men had an interest in. Do not we find, that all David's sons were in this covenant? But how many except Solomon had any right to the Covenant of Life?

The Doctrine of Baptism

Yea, Abraham himself had eight sons, and each of them a generation, but there was none of the other [who] had the Covenant of Circumcision made with them, but only Isaac, though the rest were as truly the sons of believing Abraham as Isaac was. Ishmael, and the six sons of that he had by Keturah with their generations, were all the children of the same believing Abraham as Isaac was, and yet this covenant ran not upon either of their posterity, but in Isaac saith the text, "shall thy seed be called." Though we may not be so uncharitable but to think that many of the seed of those that went into the east country might be the elect of God, and in a Covenant of Grace, yet be sure, they had not an interest in this Covenant of Circumcision, and the inheritance of Canaan.

And Isaiah tells us in Isaiah chapter 1, verse 9 that if God had not left him a very small remnant, Israel had been as Sodom and Gomorrah.

So that there was in the whole nation of Israel (that were in the Covenant of Circumcision) but a very small remnant selected out from the rest, into the Covenant of Life, as in Romans 9. The apostle so makes use of the words, and in the Romans chap 11, verse[s] 5-7, the apostle saith the election in and amongst Israel have obtained it, and the rest were hardened and blinded.

The rest (may some say), what rest? The rest of Israel in the Covenant of Circumcision by which they were, as I said, separated to God from all other nations.

But it is plain, that there was a gospel testament confirmed of God in Christ held out and tendered to the Jews by the holy prophets and penmen of God, the election obtained that, and the rest were hardened, remaining still in the literal and old Covenant of Circumcision which they had only right to by generation.

But this none could have right to but by the regeneration and new birth, and therefore saith Isaiah 8:28, "I and the children that thou hast given me are as signs and wonders" in Israel, implying clearly that a little handful of Israel are given to Christ, in the Covenant of Grace, out from amongst the body of Israel. The rest of the multitude of Israel remained without being given to Christ, making signs and wonders at such as were given to him by being admitted into a Covenant of Eternal Life through faith. It appears the whole body of Israel, were not admitted into, but some few only. So that you see souls may be in this Covenant of Circumcision, and be damned, and out of it and saved; therefore, this cannot be a Covenant of Eternal Life, but only a typical Covenant of Works.

Sixth argument to prove circumcision a Covenant of Works
The sixth ground to prove that the Covenant of Circumcision was but a covenant of works, an outward, typical covenant, was this, this Covenant of Circumcision might be broken as the Lord saith in Genesis 17:14: "And the uncircumcised man child, whose flesh of his foreskin is not circumcised, that soul shall be cut off from my people, he hath broken my covenant."

Where observe, though he were born of the family, and of the seed of Abraham, and so had an interest in the covenant; yet, he might forfeit his right, and break this covenant so as to be cast off from God's people.

This is therefore that old covenant spoke of by Jeremy[39] chapter 31, verse 31: "I will make a new covenant with the house of Israel, not like that covenant which I made with their fathers, which they broke, and my soul had no pleasure in them." For as I have shewed before, it is impossible that the New Covenant can be broken because it is an absolute covenant, made on no condition to be fulfilled by the creature, but the Lord works both to will and to do of his good pleasure, in this covenant; therefore, it is not in him that willeth, nor in him that runneth, but in

---

[39] Jeremiah.

The Doctrine of Baptism

God that shews mercy. Therefore, the Lord speaking of the new covenant in Jeremiah 33:15: and so forward saith,

> In those days and at that time, I will cause the branch of righteousness to grow up unto David, he shall execute judgement and righteousness in the land; in those days shall Judah be saved, and Jerusalem shall dwell safely, and this is the name wherewith be called, the Lord our righteousness; for thus saith the Lord, David shall never want a man to sit upon the throne of the house of Israel. Neither shall the priest, the Levite, want a man before me to offer burnt offerings, and to kindle meat offerings, and to do sacrifice continually. And the word of the Lord came to Jeremiah, saying, Thus saith the Lord, If you can break my covenant of the day, and my covenant of the night, that there should not be day and night in their seasons, then may also my covenant be broken with David my servant, that he should not have a son to reign upon his throne.

Where you see the spiritual covenant cannot be broken, as Psalm 89:34: "My covenant will I not break, nor alter the thing that is gone out of my mouth."

Therefore, it must needs be a covenant of works, that is, conditional, he made such a covenant with the priest mentioned in the first of Samuel 2:30, where the Lord saith to this purpose, "Wherefore the God of Israel said, I said indeed that thy house and the house of thy fathers should walk before me forever. But now saith the Lord, be it far from me for them that honor me, I will honor, and they that despise me, shall be lightly esteemed."

You must still mind those promises the Lord makes upon condition, the creature not walking in the performance of the condition on his part, God is set free or at liberty, whether he will perform such conditional promises, yea, or no.

But it is not so in absolute promises confirmed of God in Christ (Gal. 3:17). Those promises are all Yea, and Amen, as you see in 2 Corinthians 1:20. But the Covenant of

Circumcision, being a Covenant of Works, a poor creature truly intressed in that covenant, might break it, forfeit his interest, and be cast out and rejected out of that covenant from amongst his people, as is clearly confirmed in Isaiah 50:1: "Thus saith the Lord, where is the bill of your mother's divorcement, which I have put away, or to which of my creditors have I told you? Behold, for your iniquities have you sold yourselves, and for your transgressions is your mother put away."

Now, beloved, a divorce argues a breach and forfeiting the covenant, which the body of all Israel was in, and we know all along the national covenant was that of circumcision, and they that know in the least measure, the nature of the Covenant of Grace, cannot but know it to be such a covenant out of which a soul cannot be divorced from the Lord.

But some may say, "There are many that are visibly in a Covenant of Grace now under the Gospel, and yet may be cast out from God's people; yet, it followeth not but that it is a Covenant of Grace, and so then, they might be visibly in a Covenant of Grace, and yet be rejected."

Answer. Persons may now profess to be in Christ, and so in a Covenant of Grace, by an outward profession, but this being barely a profession, and not in truth in them that profess the same, they profess they were in that which in truth they never were. For under the Gospel, we have no infallible rule to know who is in the Covenant of Grace, and who not because we have only the confession of themselves who may deceive themselves and us.

But we have an infallible rule to judge, that Abraham, Isaac, and Jacob, and the seed forward in their loins, or their generations, were in this Covenant of Circumcision, and therefore it is a great mistake for any to evade what hath been said upon such groundless objection.

Now consider, that it is that great and faithful God that saith and professeth Abraham, his seed and family after him, from

THE DOCTRINE OF BAPTISM

Jacob forward, were in this covenant with him. But now it is only poor unfaithful man, hypocritical, dissembling, proud man, that saith he is in the Covenant of Life, when it proves not so, or when it visibly proves the contrary. For saints have a rule to disown such, But this is a most certain truth, that God did never put a soul away, and make a divorce between himself and any one soul in a Covenant of Life, and it is as certain that the whole church of Israel, were in reality and truth in the Covenant of Circumcision, as it appears in Genesis 17:10-11 where Abraham, and those born in his house, are to be circumcised. And so Psalm 105:9-11, which covenant he made with Abraham, and his oath with Isaac, and confirmed the same to Jacob by a law, and to Israel for an everlasting covenant, saying, "Unto thee have I given the land of Canaan, the lot of your inheritance."

Now it would plentifully appear (if further proof needed) that God his own self testifyeth his making and entering into covenant with Abraham, Isaac, and Jacob, and their seed forward; therefore, let no man please himself with such a poor, groundless objection. That the family of Israel were only visibly, or in the judgement of charity, in the Covenant of Circumcision as hypocrites are now in the Covenant of Grace.

For there is nothing more clear than this, that Israel were in truth and reality in the Covenant of Circumcision, expressed by the mouth of God himself, and nothing more certain that Israel were never (all of them) so much visibly in the Covenant of Grace.

For if it were necessary I could multiply places of Scripture to prove the most part of Israel visibly unbelievers, living in those manifest fruits of the flesh as drunkenness, swearing, lying, whoring, stealing, covetousness, and palpable ignorance, without faith and knowledge, shedding of blood. All these notorious sins were constantly in the greatest part of the church of Israel, that they neighed (as fed horses) after their neighbours' wives, and were given to oppression and horrid idolatry. All these sins, being such manifest fruits of the flesh, that such as live in them, the apostle saith cannot enter into the Kingdom of Christ and of God, but are visibly the children of the devil. Therefore, to say the whole body of Israel were visibly godly, and so visibly in the Covenant of Grace is a most gross mistake. They were really in the outward national Covenant of Circumcision, but not the generality so much as visibly in the gospel Covenant of Life.

For it could not be denied, but that those Jews in the 8th chapter of John verse 30, and so forward, were Abraham's children, & interessed in the Covenant of Works; yet, Christ is far from concluding that their right to the covenant of sonship, the heavenly adoption, but rather in that respect concludeth, "They are of their father the Devil, whose work they did," they being liars as he was from the beginning, and enemies to Christ as the Devil was; therefore, he excludes them from being children of God so that the main mass of blindness and darkness lying upon men's minds is this: they mix and confound the two covenants made to Abraham, the one a spiritual, heavenly covenant made to him as a father to the faithful, and to those only who walk in the steps of faithful Abraham, and the temporal Covenant of Circumcision to the seed according to the flesh from Jacob forward, and those joining themselves to that family.

So then in a word, the Covenant of Circumcision must needs be a covenant of works, and not of eternal life because it might be broken, which the covenant of eternal life cannot be.

Seventh argument to prove circumcision a Covenant of Works

The seventh ground to prove the Covenant of Circumcision not to be a covenant of grace is that if we maintain the Covenant of Circumcision to be a Covenant of Grace to eternal life, therein, we overthrow many fundamental points of religion which is strong ground to prove it is not of grace, but an outward typical

THE DOCTRINE OF BAPTISM

covenant. For it is impossible that such an understanding of Scripture which crosseth plain fundamental points of religion can be true.

Now for to give you some example for this, first, you must need confess that the Covenant of Circumcision was made to Abraham, and his seed after him in their generations, from Isaac and Jacob forward (Gen. 17:17). So that being bought with the money of one of the Israelites interessed a person in that covenant, he coming forth of that line, was born heir to that covenant and the privileges of the same.

To say that the Covenant of Grace is entailed on the flesh overthroweth the main fundamental points of our religion
Now consider, that chief and precious privileges of the Covenant of Grace are adoption or sonship, justification, and the inward work of sanctification, all which privileges that generation must needs be born heirs to if they were born heirs of a covenant of grace, which if this should be asserted, as it is by those who defend children's baptism.

Then this fundamental point of religion must needs be denied, that all mankind are by nature the children of wrath (Eph. 2:2), and that all, both Jews and Gentiles, are charged under sin, Romans 3:9: "And there is none righteous, no not one." Be it known to you, this is a fundamental doctrine of truth generally acknowledged by all the godly. "We are dead in sins and trespasses, wherein in times past we walked according to the course of this world, according to the prince of the power of the air, the spirit that now worketh in the children of disobedience, among whom also we had our conversations in times past, in the lust of the flesh, and of the mind, and were children of wrath by nature as well as others."

Now the Apostle Paul affirmeth this to be equally the state of himself who was born in the Church of Israel as well as the Gentiles; and David doth affirm this of all in general, Psalm

14:2-3, which the Apostle Paul urgeth in Rom 3:9 forwards, speaking of himself, and the rest of the national churches of the Jews, "What, are we" (saith he) "better than they?" meaning than the Gentiles. "No, in no wise," for we have before proved "that both Jews and Gentles are all under sin, as it is written, there is none righteous, no not one; there is none that understandeth, there is none that seeketh after God, they are all gone out of the way, they are together become abominable, there is none that doth good, no not one." And in Psalm 51 David saith, "I was conceived in sin, and brought forth in iniquity," who was a child of the Church of God, as it is usually termed.

But beloved, this doctrine is clear in Scripture, and clearly experienced by every godly Christian, which truth must needs be overthrown, if the whole body of Israel were born adopted sons and heirs of a covenant of eternal life, born heirs of justification, then they were never heirs of wrath, nor in a state of damnation, nor never proved nor charged under sin nor never all unrighteous, because born heirs of a Covenant of Grace, and of righteousness, nor never born dead in sin and trespasses, for that is inconsistent with being in a Covenant of Grace and Life.

This opinion of holding the covenant of grace to be entailed in the flesh, opposing itself so directly against this aforementioned foundation of religion, must needs be a gross error so considered.

The second fundamental point of religion that this error opposeth itself against is stability in a covenant of eternal life. It cannot be imagined that I should much insist upon proving this doctrine of stability in grace to be a fundamental truth, I shall take for granted from the nature of the new covenant in several scriptures before recited, as in Psalm 125, "They that trust in the Lord shall be as Mount Zion, which cannot be removed, but as the mountains are round about Jerusalem, so shall the Lord be about them from this time forth and forever." And in Psalm 89:33, "If thy children sin, I will afflict them with the rods of

The Doctrine of Baptism

men, but my loving kindness will I not utterly take from them, nor suffer my faithfulness to fail. My covenant will I not break, nor alter the thing that is gone out of my mouth."

But taking this for granted to be a truth, that all born in the Church of the Jews were born heirs of this stable covenant, and so were really and in truth in the Covenant of Grace, then most of the Church of Israel that were in a Covenant of Grace were damned, and not saved, as Isaiah 10:22–23: "Israel were as the sand of the sea, yet a remnant of them were saved only." And so Isaiah with Romans 9:27–28, 31, "But Israel which followed after the Law of righteousness, hath not obtained to the Law of righteousness." Paul saith, in Romans 11:5, "There was a remnant according to the election of grace," and in verse 7, how they obtained it, but the rest were hardened, all but the remnant were blinded, and hardened.

Therefore, [are] such multitudes, as the sand of the sea, were all really in a covenant of grace, most of them must be understood to fall out of the covenant, and so to fall out of the covenant of life.

There is another fundamental truth, that this opinion is fully against, defending that souls may be truly in a Covenant of Eternal Life, and yet perish and be damned.

The third foundation that this error overthrows is the necessity of conversion or regeneration, which doctrine is eminently confirmed by Christ in the Gospel as a fundamental truth, John 3:4–5, where Christ, speaking to Nicodemus, tells him that except a man be born again of water and of the Spirit, he cannot enter into the Kingdom of God. And likewise in John 8:24: "Except ye believe that I am he, ye shall die in your sins," and John 3, two last verses, "He that believes not, the wrath of God abideith on him, and he shall not see life."

The before mentioned error that holds a Covenant of Life running in the flesh upon the carnal seed opposeth itself against this, for might the carnal seed of Israel say to Christ, "Why do you preach such a doctrine to us, "That except you be born again, you cannot enter into the Kingdom of Heaven?" We affirm the contrary, seeing by the first birth we have an interest in the Covenant of Grace, and eternal life already, without believing or being born again, and so are entered into the Kingdom of God, and the privileges thereof. Whereas you say, "Except you believe that I am he, you shall die in your sins?" Why doth Christ pronounce death without believing, seeing we are acquainted with another way to enter into life, than the way of believing, which is to be begotten of one of the church or a believer?

We find the Holy Ghost in the 1[st epistle] of John 5 saith, "He that hath Christ hath life, he that hath not Christ hath not life." "No," saith this error. "There were thousands that were interessed in life without having Christ, that is to say, by carnal generation." Saith the apostle, "There is no other name under heaven by which we can be saved but by the name of Jesus."[40] "Yea," saith this error. "There is another name by which we may come into a covenant of eternal life, and so be saved." So that here lies the case, where Christ in the Gospel powerfully affirms no other way to life, but by believing, regeneration, and coming to Jesus Christ. This opinion destroys all these testimonies, opening another door of entrance into the covenant of life besides this, and that by fleshly generation, though Christ saith to Nicodemus, John 3, "That which is born of the flesh is flesh, and that which is born of the Spirit is Spirit," as if souls were insatiate, and had no ears to hear his plain word.

They of this opinion do defend the contrary, to what purpose should any man seek the conversion of any of believers' children, whether formerly of the nation of the Jews, or now the nations of the believing Gentles, seeing they are born heirs of a Covenant of Eternal Life, and so are in as good a state without

---

[40] Acts 4:12.

THE DOCTRINE OF BAPTISM

conversion and believing and being born again as any other soul by believing, and by new birth can be brought into?

This doctrine tends to justify the rebellious Jews against John [the] Baptist, and against Christ; the Sadducees and Pharisees came to John's baptism, Matthew 3. Saith John, "O ye generation of vipers, who hath forwarned you to fly from the wrath to come? Bring forth fruits meet for repentance, and think not to say within yourselves, we have Abraham to our Father." John, you see, would have this people to be converted to entitle them to this Covenant of Grace, and so to baptism, which is an ordinance of the same covenant, and not so much as think so erroneously as if being children to Abraham according to the flesh should entitle them to the same. Therefore, saith he, think not within yourselves, "We have Abraham to our father, and we are his children according to the flesh, and therefore we need not a work of conversion, or true repentance to entitle us to the privileges of the covenant such as baptism." And also in John 8:31, and forwards, saith Christ unto some Jews, unto whom he spake, "If you abide in my words, then are you my disciples indeed, and you shall know the truth, and the truth shall make you free, and then you shall be free indeed." They answered him, "We be Abraham's children, and were never in bondage to any. How sayest thou then, we shall be free?"

Where you may observe, these wicked, obstinate Jews were of the same opinion, that they were in a state of happiness good enough by generation by being Abraham's seed according to the flesh. Jesus answereth, "Whoso committeth sin is the servant of sin, and the servant abideth not in the house forever." We find Christ afterwards tells these sons of Abraham, that they were so far from being the adopted sons of God in a covenant of life that they were of their father the devil, and these same persons Christ speaks to in verse the 24th, telling them except they believed Christ was he, they should die in their sins.

Christ was far from this opinion as to think that Covenant of Circumcision to be a Covenant of Life, but he doth thoroughly reprehend them for this groundless confidence. This error was the main obstacle that hindered the Jews from faith and repentance because they thought it entitled them to happiness enough to be of the stock of Abraham, and to be born heirs of the Covenant of Circumcision. This very rotten opinion was to them one of the devil's sleights to lull them asleep in a carnal and unconverted condition. They thought that needed not which thought of theirs had been true enough, provided all the children of Abraham had, by generation, interest in the Covenant of Life, which other men could have no interest in without regeneration. But Christ you see presseth a necessity of conversion to these children of Abraham that at the present were as fully interessed in the Covenant of Circumcision as Abraham that at the present were as fully interessed in the Covenant of Circumcision as Abraham himself even to Nicodemus which was a ruler of the Jews, Christ presseth a necessity thereof to him, and also labours by a parable in Luke 16 to convince those sottish Jews that one might be the seed of Abraham according to the flesh, and yet be irrevocably damned, and therefore he brings in the rich man in hell, speaking thus, "Father Abraham, I pray thee, send Lazarus to dip the tip of his finger in water to cool my tongue. And Abraham is brought in, owning him to be his son, speaking thus, My son, remember, that thou in thy life time, receivedest thy good things."

Where you may observe, that the man in hell, irrecoverably damned, owns Abraham to be his Father, and Abraham also doth acknowledge him to be his son, "My son," saith Abraham, where you clearly see a man may be a son of Abraham, and yet be damned. "Thou hadst thy good thing in this life, but Lazarus his evil things." Ezekiel 18:9-10, where a just man is presupposed to beget a son that is a robber, and a shedder of blood, and that goes out in all manner of wickedness, and that in Israel.

Wherein observe, Abraham owns no other privilege belonged to the rich man by virtue of being the son of Abraham, but was in his life, or in this world. Hell was his best portion in the world to come, which if he had been born heir to the Covenant of Life, how then could Abraham's affirmation have been true?

Beloved, let all ingenuous spirits that are not willing to walk blind-fold[ed], consider how contrary to the whole tenor of the Gospel this opinion is. Consider how destructive to this fundamental principle of the Gospel, the necessity of Christ, of regeneration. This opinion destroys all sense of the necessity of conversion, and helps to harden men to destruction, as it did the blind Jews, who, (as it appears) were fully blinded in the receipt of that opinion, that being Abraham's seed according to the flesh, interessed them in happiness and eternal life.

Fourthly, this opinion destroys the doctrine of the New Covenant, and the nature of it, and the manner of God's making of it with the soul. For to make a new covenant with the soul is to write the Law of God in a man's heart, and in his mind, and to infuse saving knowledge and faith by which God unites the soul to himself, and so pardons all his sins, and without any condition considered in the creature, binds over himself to be their God freely in Christ, and binds over himself to his own them to be his people. And only thus, and no otherwise, is God said to make his new covenant with a poor soul. Whereas this dream would seem to bear you in hand, that a whole nation may be in a new covenant, and have it made with them, and yet have none of all this work wrought in their hearts.

Fifthly, this opinion destroys the doctrine of justification by faith in Christ, only seeing that it doth hold out another way than by faith to come to justification, which is by carnal birth of believing parents; for if a soul be admitted into a Covenant of Life, I hope you are not ignorant that justification is a great privilege in the new covenant, and really the portion of all that are in that covenant.

Sixthly, this opinion destroys the doctrine and foundation of all gospel churches where it is held which will appear by two things.

First, it destroys the matter of the Church. You know that this is a fundamental truth, that the matter of the Church ought (now under the Gospel) to be "saints by calling" (1 Cor. 1:2); "spiritual worshipers" (John 4:23); "lively stones" (1 Pet. 2:5); "Such as are redeemed from their vain conversation" (1 Pet. 1:18); "Such brought out of darkness into his marvelous light" (1 Pet. 2:9).

Now this error destroys the truth, or opposeth itself against the truth of God, lying in all these scriptures, it brings in the nation of believers, all born of their body, their seed's seed in their generation, if you will be faithful to this principle, whereon this seems to be grounded. For the Covenant of Circumcision was not only to the next generation immediately flowing from Abraham, But to thy seed after thee in their generations: And we see in that generation in Christ's time, they were as well called Abraham's seed as Isaac himself was, and they did call Abraham their father.

Therefore if the Covenant of Circumcision shall be man's pattern, we must necessarily have a church that is national, consisting of succeeding generations for many hundred years coming out of believing persons' loins, and so set up the partition wall again between the natural branches, and those that are wild by nature. So that this tenet doth of necessity destroy the true matter of a church because it unavoidably admits into the Church all the unconverted and unregenerate children born of the bodies of such persons, that either are or have been accounted believers.

And as it destroys the matter of a church in admitting such that are not made disciples, so it occasions such as do believe, remaining in that opinion to live in that sin of neglect of the Lord's baptism, contenting themselves with that counterfeit of baptism which they had in their infancy. So that this evil opinion occasions the constitution of a church or congregation of good and bad promiscuously, and all these unbaptized both the good and the bad. What light in the gospel have you to justify such an assembly to be the true Church in Christ that doth consist of some religious people in the judgment of charity, and a world of carnal children admitted and received among them, and all both the carnal and the religious never baptized with the Lord's baptism?

I do deny such an assembly can be owned an orderly church of Christ. Thus you see, what a great error this is that opposeth itself against so many fundamental points of the Gospel.

But may some say though we receive in children by baptism into our church, we do not admit them unto the Supper. The question is when you will admit them? See what an untrodden path you are run into. Do you own your children to be in a covenant of grace, and eternal life, and inrighted into the privileges of the same? And is baptism the privilege of the New Covenant, and not the Supper also? If it be, how dare you keep them from their right and privilege, I pray you? How long did the apostles baptize their members before they admitted them to the Supper?

If you look in Acts 2:41-42, you shall find so many as gladly received the word of God were baptized, and presently they continued in the apostles' doctrine, fellowship, breaking of bread, and prayer, as soon as they were baptized.

Therefore, you have no ground at all upon any pretense to suspend such members that you own privileged in all the ordinances of God from the Supper which you have received into your church by your supposed baptism.

Thus, you may see, what horrible consequences flow naturally from the maintaining a Covenant of Eternal Life in the flesh.

Seventhly, this opinion defends another gross error, that persons may have right to a Covenant of Life without union or in-being in Christ by faith. It is a sad thing that souls profess knowledge in the Gospel, and to be preachers of the same, should be so blinded thus to mislead people in so weighty a point as this is, and that should endeavor to leaven thousands of poor people with such a sad error that opposeth itself against the very substance of the Gospel in holding all the whole nation of Israel to be in a Covenant of Eternal Life, and also the carnal children of believing parents among the Gentiles, though they had no union by faith in Christ, the greatest part of them.

Somewhat offered to prove that presently upon the fall made an outward carnal covenant entailed upon the flesh
I come to the third thing, which is to prove that the Covenant of Eternal Life never was, nor shall be made with any but such as believe, or such as are in Christ. For the better clearing of that, you must understand that as soon as the seed of the woman was promised, to wit, Christ Jesus, which was the whole of the New Covenant, all promises being Yea and Amen, spiritual and heavenly blessings being given in him, this being one main point then to be made known to the sons of men, that he must come out of the woman. You must, I say, understand that the Lord did presently make and outward covenant, which was typical, entailed upon the flesh out of which the Messiah should come.

But I must confess, this is not held forth so clearly till the time of Abraham, nor then so clear, as it was afterwards by the hands of Moses. But it was clear to me that in substance the same covenant of ceremonial obedience, which was given to Moses when the people came out of Egypt, the same was given to Adam's generation, upon the promise of Christ, which was

THE DOCTRINE OF BAPTISM

to go on in the fleshly line, out of which Christ was to come, and this to continue, till he did come in the flesh, and then to cease. The reason that induceth me thus to judge is this:

I find Cain and Abel at the end of the year of days bring their sacrifice, and the one brought the firstlings of the flock, and the fat thereof. Thus did God command the same things to Israel by Moses (Exod. 34:19; 13: 12-13). And you see Cain brought the first fruits of the ground, and we find this delivered by Moses, as part of the covenant to the Jews in Deuteronomy 18:4, and 26:2. For saith the Lord, "Thou shalt bring all of the first fruits of the Earth, which thou shalt bring of thy land that the Lord thy God gives thee" (Mic. 7:1; Lev. 2:12, 14; Prov. 3:19).

Though ye do not here see from what rule Cain and Abel did thus do, yet we must take for granted, they had it from God. How else could Abel have performed his worship acceptably if he had not a ground to do it by faith, and it is certain he did it in faith; therefore, had he rule for the same (as Heb. 11:4). And we find that in that time, there was a distinction of clean and unclean beasts that went into the Ark.

Now what cleanses or uncleanses is here meant by virtue of a law; for certainly that law which God gave to forbid such beasts and creatures was that which made one clean, and not another, and this law was by Moses delivered in Leviticus 11; spoke of to Peter Acts 10: "Call not thou unclean what God hath made clean" and likewise eating blood is forbidden (Gen. 9:4), or flesh with the life thereof. The same Moses gave [in] Leviticus 17:10-11, where blood is forbidden upon the same ground and reason.

We find in Genesis 6:5 that God hints at a sin of the old world, for which he brought the flood, which was that "the sons of God married the daughters of men, seeing they were fair," which must needs be understood, there was a law prohibiting Seth's posterity to marry Cain's. This law was also given by Moses in Deuteronomy 7:2-3. We must of necessity understand, these laws were from God to Adam, and so to his sons, and so in substance the same was given to Abraham with some additions, and same by Moses, committed to writing with further additions, but this is the result, that I would come to: God, having promised the seed of the woman to come out of that flesh, did institute an external covenant of worship, that the Lord did carry all along upon the flesh, the Word would be incarnate, I understand upon the first promise of Christ to Adam and Eve, God then made this ceremonial covenant of worship with Adam's family; therefore, both his sons were trained up as worshipers, and this must needs be, because Cain was never in a covenant of grace, nor we have no ground to judge that he had ever any appearance of true grace in him; but God, having no intent to bring his promised seed out of Cain or Abel, upon which he rejects Cain, with all his posterity, as a fugitive and a vagabond. From what did he reject him, but from this church covenant of ceremonial obedience and worship? But when Seth was born, God (as it appears to me) did renew a fresh election upon him, and his seed according to the flesh, and the whole race of Seth were God's Church. God hereby teaching, that the Messiah must come out of that family according to the flesh, and not out of Cain's or his posterity, nor any other.

And when God had destroyed the world by the flood, then there was only Noah's family, consisting of eight persons, being all of them in this church covenant of worship for a time till God pitched a fresh election upon Shem by the mouth of Noah his father (Gen. 9:26). Herein is the election where Ham and Japheth, with their posterities, are passed by, though as truly the seed of believing Noah to Shem was passed. And this ceremonial Covenant of Works goes on upon Shem till the time of Abraham. The world growing then numerous, God would have his Church in a more narrow compass, and more especially take unto him that particular family out of which Christ should come, which was Abraham. So that by the way observe.

The Doctrine of Baptism

The main ground upon which God elects Abraham's family into the outward covenant with himself, and not Lot's, nor any of the rest of the godly families then living in the world. It was not because Abraham was any more a believer or his family the family of a believer; for if so, then Lot, and his family, and all the godly men's families in the world, had been necessarily taken into the Covenant of Circumcision because they and their families had been believers as well as Abraham's. This is a sure rule, if God gives a promise or a command to any person, considered in such a capacity as a believer, then whosoever is a believer, that command and promise belongs unto them. I might by manifold instances clear this, as when God saith to Joshua, "I will not leave thee nor forsake thee," this being not made to him under any other consideration but as a believer.

Why the Covenant of Circumcision is made to Abraham and his seed and not to others
The apostle is bold to say, the promise is made to the whole Church of the Hebrews (Heb. 12:5), they being all believers as Joshua was, but this Covenant of Circumcision now so termed was made with Abraham, his seed, and family, and not upon this ground, because he was a believer, but because that Christ must come out of his flesh and line. Therefore, the work is to confirm and ratify this to Abraham, that Christ should so come, and to point out to all the world where they must look for and expect the Christ. God doth as much as say, in Abraham's loins you must expect him, and nowhere else. For as Christ saith to the woman of Samaria, "The Jews know what they worship, for salvation is of the Jews;"[41] therefore, to be sure, the covenant of worship runs in that line.

But now Abraham had eight sons, the one by Sarah (Gen. 21:2); the other by Hagar (Gen. 16); and six sons by his wife Keturah (Gen. 25:1, 26), to which he gave gifts, and sent away to

---
[41] John 4:22.

the East Country from his son Isaac, and this Covenant of Works did belong only to Isaac and his seed. For when God had, in Genesis 11:17, 7, promised that he would be the God of Abraham, and his seed in their generations, and give them Canaan, in the conclusion of this covenant he begins to speak to Abraham of a son he should have by Sarah, and that she should be the Mother of Nations, as in Hebrews 11. Abraham, being affected with his son, Ishmael, which he then enjoined, saith, "O that Ishmael might live in thy sight", as if Abraham should say, "Lord I understand that thou hast made a church covenant with me, and my seed after me, taking my seed in their generations into external covenant with thee, O (as if he should say) that Ishmael might be the seed upon which the covenant might run." Here God tells Abraham that he had heard his prayer, that he would bless Ishmael with manifold outward blessings otherwise, but, saith he, "my covenant shall be with Isaac", meaning here, that outward Covenant of Circumcision, where you have Ishmael, and the six sons of Keturah with all their posterity passed by, in this fresh election of Isaac and his seed, which were only elected in this covenant.

Therefore, the bond-child, and the six sons of Keturah, though as truly believers' children, as Isaac was, yet, they are all dismissed [from] this covenant and privileges of the same.

The six sons of Keturah, as you have heard before, Abraham gave them gifts, and sent them into the East Country. And when Isaac had two sons in Rebecca's womb, God again made a fresh election of Jacob, and his seed in their generations, passing by Esau, and his seed; for saith God, "There are two nations in thee, and two peoples."[42] So he chose Jacob, considered as a nation, and passed by Esau, considered as another nation. For it is plain from those words, "there are two nations, and two peoples," that the election was a national election, and a national

---

[42] Genesis 25:23.

The Doctrine of Baptism

rejection. He saith, "The elder shall serve the younger."[43] This saying, "The elder shall serve the younger," is interpreted by Malachi 1 to be a loving of Jacob, and a hating of Esau, laying his mountain waste, that is, his church power privilege, that he seemingly had expected to have been heir of, and the loving of Jacob, is meant the external electing love in the Covenant of Circumcision, according that in Deuteronomy 7:7, speaking to the whole nation, "The Lord did not set his love upon you, nor chide you, because you were more in number than any people, for you were the fewest of all people, but because the Lord loved."

This election and this love is equal alike to the whole nation of Israel; therefore, so considered, you must mind, this is, as I said before, only an external election of Jacob, and these in his lines, into the national Covenant of Circumcision, as before in Genesis 18. He saith, "In Isaac shall thy seed be called." The meaning, as the 17th chapter expounds, is this: that the seed in their generations, that God would continue the Covenant of Circumcision upon, was that seed which was to come out of Isaac, and not that which came out of Ishmael, and the six sons of Keturah, none of them or their seed, were to be of that great nation which God promised to make of Abraham; for the Lord saith to Abraham, "I will make a mighty nation out of thee," (Gen. 18:18).

Now by "this nation" you must understand is meant the national church taken into the Covenant of Circumcision, whereas in the spiritual covenant all the nations were to be blessed in him, and he is to be the father of multitudes of nations (Gen. 12:3; 17:4-5). But this Covenant of Circumcision must not relate to any but those that came out of Isaac with his family, and then those that came out of the loins of Jacob with his family though this be a true literal interpretation of those texts and really the proper mind of God, yet there is a mystical and spiritual

---

[43] Genesis 25:23.

sense pointed and driven at, which Paul, that infallible apostle, did clearly give out from those texts in Romans 9. That as Isaac typed out Christ, so this temporal seed elected in Isaac typed out this spiritual election in Christ. The temporal seed in a temporal covenant elected in Jacob points out the choice of Christ and all his seed into a spiritual covenant.

So a spiritual election in these texts was typed and figured out as the apostle doth clearly maintain, the apostles not being ministers of the letter, but the Spirit (2 Cor. 3). But most true it is, that Jacob, and the whole nation elected with him, were elected into an outward covenant, and Esau and his seed were not, but were refused and passed by. And consider now in the womb was Jacob and his posterity any more the seed of a believer, than Esau and his seed were? Sure it is, he was not. Therefore, away with that error taken for granted that the Covenant of Circumcision was made to believers and their seed.

This Covenant of Circumcision you may clearly see was not made to Abraham nor to his seed considered as a believer's, but upon this ground or reason that the Messiah was to come of Abraham, not of Lot. The Messiah was to come out of Isaac, and not of Ishmael, nor of the six sons of Keturah, and Christ was to come out of Jacob and his posterity, and not out of Esau. Here you may nakedly see how greatly they mistake that think the covenant was made to Abraham and his seed considered as believers and believers' seed.

If a national covenant was made with Abraham and his seed according to the flesh out of which flesh the Messiah was to come, and that upon this reason then you cannot conclude that the covenant can belong to any Gentile and his seed upon the same ground. Therefore if you would tell where to find a Gentile now among many others that were to have Christ to come out of his loins according to the flesh, then you would have the same ground to say that in like manner a church covenant should run upon him and his seed until Christ were come out of that flesh or line.

But when Christ was come and fully exhibited in the flesh, then the ground upon which this covenant was given, being ceased, the covenant also ceaseth.

To defend a covenant of life entailed on the flesh is virtually to deny that Christ is come in the flesh
Therefore for any man to go about to defend a covenant in the flesh, it is a doctrine virtually denying the Christ is come and fully manifested in the flesh.

Therefore you may from all that hath been spoken draw this conclusion: that there was never a covenant of eternal life made with any but with such as did and do believe, all along till Christ not since.

Therefore see that objection answered, that the spiritual privileges are not less under the Gospel than under the Law, though we deny all the carnal generation to have any right to the Covenant of Grace or privileges thereof, both then and now. The offers and tenders of the Gospel we must confess were to that nation, and in that sense, they were called the children of the prophets, and of the covenant (Acts 3), and latter end, and in their respect now the privileges are larger because all nations are in the same sense the children of the prophets, and of the covenant now, since Christ came, the prophet and minister of God, having commission now to publish the Gospel or New Covenant to all nations

7
None Have Right in the Covenant of Grace but Such as Are United by Christ in Faith

But further, to prove that none have right to a Covenant of Grace or Life, but such as had and have union with Christ by faith is most plain.

First, because as you have heard, the New Covenant was confirmed of God in Christ only. Galatians 3:17: "And all the promises are in Christ, yea and Amen."

Therefore this covenant cannot belong to any soul out of Christ, because they are "Yea and Amen." 1 Corinthians 11:25: "This cup is the New Testament in my blood," saith Christ. If the New Testament be in Christ's blood, then what hath any carnal or unbelieving wretch to do with this Testament that have not faith in his blood?

And further we do find in Matthew 3:17. The Lord saith, "This is my beloved Son in whom I am well pleased." Mark the words, "in whom;" then to be sure out of him he is not well pleased, that is, in respect to this especial well-pleasedness, or electing love in the Covenant of Life, according to that in Ephesians 1:6: "He hath made us accepted in the Beloved." Out of the beloved there can be no acceptation. Therefore it is said, "God accepted" Abel "and the offering" (Gen. 4:4). The author to the Hebrews, 6:11:4 tells you, Abel "by faith offered a more acceptable or excellent sacrifice than Cain, by which he obtained witness that he was righteous. So by faith in the promised seed he came to be righteous and accepted of God as you have heard" in Ephesians 1:3: "God hath blessed us with all spiritual, and heavenly blessings in heavenly things in Christ Jesus." Therefore, no heavenly or spiritual blessing can belong to any out of Christ. "For in Adam all die, so in Christ shall all be made alive." There is none made alive but those that are in

Christ; for the wicked men's resurrection is not said to be to life, but to damnation (1 Cor. 15:21[-22] with John 5:28-29). "And therefore in thee shall all the nations of the earth be blessed" (Gen. 18:18), must imply thus much, that out of Christ the true seed all nations should be accursed (Gen. 12:3 with 22:18; Gal. 3:8). I must confess it is a sad thing that at such a time of the world as this where the means of grace and knowledge of the Gospel hath been so plentifully held forth, that we must be forced to bestow such pains to prove that men cannot be in a state of salvation and acceptation before God in a covenant of grace without union in Christ by faith. But however, considering that the apostle saith, there is no other name under heaven by which we can be saved but by the name of Jesus, and a particular faith in him (Acts 4:12), and therefore Peter saith in John 6:69, "Whether shall we go? Thou hast the words of eternal life" he is the "way, the truth, and the life" (John 14:6). There is none [who] can come into the Father's love and mercy, nor into the covenant of life, or any spiritual privilege, but by him, he is the "narrow way that leads to life, and few there be that find it" (Matt. 7:14). Therefore, saith the apostle, "He that hath Christ hath life, but he that hath not Christ hath not life;" but all the carnal unbelieving children from the foundation of the world unto this day have not Christ; therefore, not life, that is to say, nor the covenant of life, nor the justification of life, which every man must needs have, that is in the covenant of life. We find that all patriarchs and holy men of God, by faith and patience, inherited the promises, and not by generation (Heb. 6:12; 11:12); therefore, sprang there, even of one, and him as good as dead, so many as the stars in the sky for multitude, and as the sand which is by the sea shore, innumerable, these all died in faith.

This text speaks of that spiritual and believing seed of Abraham, which he considered as believing and faithful, Abraham was the father of, according to Genesis 15:5-6, "so shall thy seed be."

Secondly, it further appears that the covenant of eternal life was never made with any but such as believe because all unbelievers, both of Jews and Gentiles are charged under sin (Rom. 3:9), and have the wrath of God abiding on them last. Yea though of the seed of Israel and children of that Covenant of Circumcision, to them Christ saith, "Except ye believe that I am he, you shall die in your sins" (John 8:24). And the Gospel tells the national church of the Jews, that those of them that believed not were condemned already because they believed not in the only begotten Son of God (John 3:18).

Which clearly proves that none of them were in a covenant of life by generation, for if they had, then the want of conversion would not have damned them, nor left them in a state of damnation.

Further, doth not Christ himself, call and account the unbelieving Jews the world when he saith to his disciples, "If you were of the world, the world would love his own, but because you are not of the world, but I have chosen you out of the world, therefore the world hates you?" And this world that Christ chooseth his disciples out of, and that hated his disciples as they had formerly hated him, are but the nation of the Jews that were in that Covenant of Circumcision which plainly proves that all unbelievers in that nation were the world, and therefore not in a covenant of grace.

And again it must needs be so because the apostle saith in Romans 4:16: "Therefore it is of faith that it might be by grace to the end that the promise might be sure to all the seed."

Observe from the text, if the promise, or covenant, or any spiritual privilege should be entailed upon the flesh, or conveyed any way then by faith, it could not be by grace.

And again, faith is the first differencing grace, to difference God's people from all other (Acts 15:9), and put no difference between us and them, purifying their hearts by faith; therefore, it is impossible the Covenant of Grace can be made to any other but such as have faith. And again, I find none counted the spiritual seed of Abraham unto whom the Covenant of Life belongs, but them that are in Christ by faith, as Galatians 3:28-29 [says]: "There is neither Jew nor Gentile, there is neither bond nor free, neither male nor female, for you are all one in Christ Jesus, and if you be in Christ, then are you Abraham's seed, and heirs according to the promise." The same in Romans 4:14: "If they which were of the Law be heirs, faith is made void, and the promise made of none effect," meaning thereby the Covenant of Circumcision, as appears in the ver[se] 10 & 11. And so in Romans 9:7-8: "Not because they are the seed of Abraham are they all children, but in Isaac shall thy seed be called," that is, they which are the children of the flesh, they are not the children of God, but the children of the promise, are counted for the seed.

Where you see, that the apostle doth deny that seed of Abraham that were only his children according to the flesh to be the spiritual seed, but such as are born of promise or begotten by promise, they are accounted for the seed chosen in him, and united to him by faith.

These were pointed and figured out by the national and temporal seed, that came out of the loins of Isaac, those souls there born in the house, and brought with money were in the outward covenant and privileges, but these regenerate and born again by promise, are the heavenly seed. So the heavenly generation are such only born from above, and this is that the Psalmist speaks of in Psalm 22:30: "A seed shall serve him, and it shall be accounted to him for a generation."

For the temporal Israel, and the typical election of them into the temporal covenant, did point out this spiritual election in a spiritual covenant, confirmed of God in Christ Jesus.

Further, it appears that none but such as believe are in a covenant of grace because without faith it is impossible to please God (Heb. 11:6). Therefore, Abel by faith had his person and offering accepted (Gen. 4:4), but Cain, and his offering being not in faith, God accepted not, for all the thoughts of such a man are only evil, and that continually till they believe, as Genesis 6:5 and 8:21 [say]. All the imaginations of all believers till converted are evil, and only evil continually.

Secondly, they are evil, Mathew 12:34: "O generation of vipers, how can you being evil speak good word[s], for out of the abundance of the heart the mouth speaketh, an evil man out of the evil treasure of his heart brings forth evil things," and as their thoughts and words are evil, so in like manner, their actions are all evil, natural actions, as eating, Job 20:23: "When he is eating to fill his belly, God shall cast the fury of his wrath upon him and shall rain it upon him while he is eating;" thus you see natural actions are evil, such as eating and drinking for satisfying his hunger, and also civil actions are evil, as Proverbs 21:4: "An high look, and a proud heart, and the ploughing of the wicked is sin"; if plowing, then all his civil actions, and also his best duties of worship, as his sacrifice, is an abomination to God (Prov. 8:9, 15:8; Isa. 1; 66:4). Upon this ground it must needs be that the Covenant of Grace and Eternal Life cannot belong to any such persons that do not believe, for it is impossible to be in a Covenant of Grace, and yet not to have persons nor any of their best actions accepted.

Yea further, all mankind are compared to beasts, till they believe, Job 11:11: "Vain man would fain be wise, but man is born like a wild ass' colt" (with Jer. 2:23-24). Yea the Lord saith in Revelation 21:8, that "the fearful, and unbelieving, and the abominable, and murderers, and whoremongers, and sorcerers, and idolaters, and all liars shall have their portion in the lake which burneth with fire and brimstone, which is the second death."

Beloved, therefore if any have been so deluded as to believe such a notorious error as this is, to think that any ever hath been in the Covenant of Life, but such as are in Christ by faith, I desire God may give you repentance for maintaining such a fundamental error as this is.

8
Answers to Such Scriptures as Alleged to Prove the Baptism of Infants

And now in the fourth place, I shall endeavour to answer such Scripture allegations, and those especially brought in from the New Testament to countenance this error, wherein I shall endeavor to take off those false and corrupt glosses that are usually put upon them, wherein men pretend to prove the Covenant of Grace among the Gentiles, to run in the flesh and line of believing parents under the Gospel, which I am sure was never yet since the world began, nor never shall be with any neither parents nor children, but such individual persons that particularly believed in Christ with their own hearts.

An answer to that text Acts 2:39
And first let me speak to that in Acts 2:39, which is usually pretended to be proof of the covenant in the flesh. The words are these: "The promise is to you and to your children, and to all that are afar off, even as many as the Lord our God shall call." Now I pray you take notice how evident this text makes against this error. For this text affirms only the promises to belong to so many even as God shall call, and that is a fundamental truth, if by promise you understand the gift of the Holy Ghost, or remission of sins, or both, to be promised in this text.

It is most true, that so many as God shall call have an interest, both to Christ and all the promises in him, and only they, for saith the text, "Repent and be baptized every one of you for the remission of sins, and ye shall receive the Holy Ghost." So that [you may have] remission of sins and the gift of the Holy Ghost, it is safe to understand here to be meant that promise that is said to belong to them, to their children, and to those afar off, even so many of them, and their children, and those afar off, as the Lord our God should call; agreeable to the words thus understood is Romans 8:30: "Moreover whom he called, them he also justified, and whom he justified, them he also glorified," so that justification, or remission of sins, is here given only to called persons. Likewise, these agreeth that of Hebrews 9:15: "For this cause he is the mediator of the New Testament, that by means of death, for the redemption of the transgression that were under the first testament, they which are called might receive the promise of the eternal inheritance." So here you see that those that are predestinated to have a Covenant of Life, and the blessing given in that covenant, are first called, as 1 Peter 2:9: "He hath called us out of darkness into his marvelous light." Now this text is plain, to prove that those Jews and proselytes that then heard him and their children, and also the ten tribes now afar off, and also the Gentiles, the promises did belong to so many of all these as God should call, and except souls be given up to a spirit of delusion, will nay dare affirm that the promises of the Spirit, remission of sins, and eternal life do belong to any other? Will any be so ignorant as to judge, that those promises did belong to the generation of the Jews whether they were called or not, though they continued in unbelief and hardness of heart and impenitency? Is not such a corrupt interpretation against Christ's words to that very people? John 8:24: "Except you believe that I am he, you shall die in your sins," speaking to these very Jews. Doth not John the Baptist say to these (John 3:36), "He that believeth not the Son shall not see life, but the wrath of God abideth on him?" [He was] directing this speech indefinitely to the generation of the Jews, the seed of Abraham, such as were in the Covenant of Circumcision.

But if by "the children" you understand, so many of them as God should call, whether then at that time, or afterwards to the end of the world, it is most true that to such of their children the promise of grace did belong.

The Doctrine of Baptism

But beloved, the Scripture is in nothing more full than this, that the promise of grace belonged not to any of those Jews' seed, but such as were called, for God shuts them under unbelief, and because of unbelief they were broken off (Rom. 11). If unbelief excluded them from that eternal relation, which before Christ's death, they then had in the covenant entailed on the flesh, and Christ coming in the flesh, and fully exhibiting and putting an end to that covenant, no other covenant standing in force in the Church of God but what Christ was the mediator of, these unbelieving Jews of necessity were broken off. The promise of remission of sins was so far from running upon the unbelieving Jews, the true fleshly seed of Abraham, the Apostle Paul affirms the contrary, Acts 19:9: "But when divers were hardened, and believed not, but spake evil of that way before the multitude, he departed from them;" and Acts 13:45-46:

> But when the Jews saw the multitude, they were filled with envy, and spake against those things that were spoken by Paul, contradicting and blaspheming, then Paul and Barnabas, waxed bold, and said, 'It was necessary that the word of God should first have been spoken to you, but seeing ye put it from you and judge yourselves unworthy of everlasting life? Lo, we turn to the Gentiles, for so hath the Lord commanded us.'

See also verse 50: "The Jews stirred up the devout and honorable women, and raised persecution against Paul and Barnabas," but it should seem to be the general understanding of those that urge this text for a covenant in the flesh, that if they were the seed of the Jews, though they were not called, nor did not believe, but were hardened in their continuance in unbelief, yet this promise of remission of sins, and the gift of the Holy Ghost belongs to them. This interpretation, that this text must have to defend a covenant in the flesh, which I leave to any intelligent man to consider, how greatly erroneous it is to affirm that the promise of the remission of sins belongs to the unbelieving and hardened children of the Jews, that God hath not, nor doth call. So that you may clearly see that the truth lies in this text, that the promise is no more of fathers nor children, nor those afar off but such as God, by his especial grace, doth call to be the sons of God by faith.

An answer to that text 1 Corinthians 7:14
Another Scripture made use of, or rather abused and wrested to defend this error is 1 Corinthians 7:14: "The unbelieving husband is sanctified by the believing wife, and the unbelieving wife is sanctified by the believing husband, else were your children unclean, but now are they holy," whence is gathered by those of that opinion, that this holiness is (as they call it) a federal holiness, or a covenant holiness, that is to say, God, having taken the believing parent with the child into covenant with himself, the child is in this sense holy, that is covenant holy.

Now for the better understanding this text, I pray consider how, and in what sense, God takes persons into covenant with himself; and that as you have heard is two ways; either he takes souls to himself in a typical covenant. He took Israel to himself in that covenant, and in that sense they may be said to be separated from the rest of the world, which separation of them from the rest of the world to himself is a holiness that the carnal Jew was only partaker of, such a typical and legal holiness, that people being separated from all other nations in the world to God in this covenant. Now the word, "holy," signifies so much as separating or setting apart, and in this sense the vessels of the temple were holy as also the priests, being by law set apart from the rest of Israel to offer the bread of their God.

Now in the 2nd place, there is also a New Covenant or a Covenant of Life that God takes a people to himself, which is to write his law in their hearts, & in their minds, to sanctify the[m] and to justify them. Now this internal holiness which God as an effect of that covenant infuseth into the heart, is only this New

THE DOCTRINE OF BAPTISM

Covenant holiness; for there is no other holiness that relates to the New Covenant; when the heart and the inward man shall be purified through faith. And when the whole heart and affections are by the powerful work of God's grace, separated from sin, and those vanities below to heaven and heavenly things, this is the only holiness that the covenant of eternal life conveys to souls. The hypocrite may have this in appearance, but the elect and chosen have this only in truth. He puts no difference between us and them, purifying our hearts by faith, and he hath by one offering for ever perfected them that are sanctified (Heb. 10). This sanctification of the Spirit and belief of the truth goes always together (2 Thess. 2:13). Therefore, it is impossible that this should be the meaning of the text, that all believers' carnal seed are in a covenant of eternal life, and so have their hearts purified and sanctified through the work of the Spirit and faith, before they are born, and in this sense are born holy.

I know no other sanctification the Scripture speaks of belonging to a covenant of grace and eternal life, and for the external or typical holiness in an outward covenant it cannot be, because that was abolished through Christ's death, as appears in Hebrews chapters 8, 9; therefore, far be it from the apostles to intend here the countenancing of any such erroneous opinion as that every believer's child was by virtue of his first birth, internally holy with that holiness of truth, as the apostle calls it (Eph. 4:24).

If you please, therefore hearken to the true meaning of the text, which is to this effect: The Corinthians, having sent several doubts and questions to the apostle to resolve and answer, as appears in the first verse of this chapter, he answereth them particularly, and it seems among the rest, they had a Jewish question started, grounded (as we suppose) upon Ezra 9, [and] Deuteronomy 7:2 where you find it was unlawful for a Jew to marry with a stranger. Therefore, Ezra caused all those men that had taken them strange wives to put them away as not lawfully married because such was contrary and against the Law given to them. They were to put them away, and the children born of them as illegitimate and unclean in an unlawful fellowship.

These Corinthians it seems, did propound in writing to the apostle this question, whether such of them as had unbelieving husbands and wives yet remaining in idolatry might lawfully abide with them in that fellowship in the marriage-bed, and whether that fellowship were not unclean and unlawful, as in Ezra's time?

Unto this question the apostle answers [in] verse 12: "To the rest speak I, not the Lord. If any brother hath a wife that believeth not, and she be pleased to dwell with him, let him not but her away, and the woman which hath a husband which believeth not, and if he be pleased to dwell with her, let her not leave him." But also might they say, "Why is not our marriage fellowship unclean?" Therefore, in verse 14 saith he, "The unbelieving wife is sanctified (as the Geneva translation hath it[44]) to the believing husband, or else were your children unclean, but now are they holy." As if Paul should say, the reason why I would have the believing husband to abide with the unbelieving wife is this, because the unbeliever (now since the partition-wall is down between Jew and Gentile) may justifiably be a wife to a believing husband, there being now no law in the New Testament against such marriages, especially considering their marriage was transacted, when they were both idolatrous heathen.

Now it being taken for granted their marriage was lawful in these words, "The unbelieving wife is sanctified to the believing husband," and that it be understood, that the unbelieving husband is, by the law of marriage sanctified to, or set apart or separated to, or made holy to the believing wife, the law of marriage, having separated him from all other women in the world to be to her, and her only, else were your children unclean.

---

[44] Geneva Bible (1560).

The Doctrine of Baptism

"Mark," saith the apostle, "else were your children unclean, but now are they holy," that is, if the Law of God did not set the unbeliever apart to the believer, and so justify their fellowship in the marriage bed, then would the children begotten in that fellowship be unclean and base born, but now they are holy, that is, now they are begotten in holy wedlock according to the holy law of marriage, not as those children were in Ezra's time which were unclean. So that from the unbeliever's lawful and sanctified abode with the believer, doth the apostle conclude the children to be clean or holy. And thus all children of heathen are in the same holy, that are begotten in holy wedlock, for as the fellowship of man and woman in the bed being not according to the Law is called fornication, uncleanness, and unholiness, so the fellowship of any two persons, even of heathen, being according to that law of marriage, it is then clean or holy, and so the children begotten in that fellowship, are said to be clean or holy begotten in that fellowship, are said to be clean or holy begotten. But there was none doubted of the holiness of the heathen, they never having any law to prohibit their marriage together, but now the Jews, having an express law against marrying with any other nation, it was legally unclean or unholy to match with any such, or to bed with any such that were not Jews, or proselytes.

Now that law you must mind was part of the partition-wall between Jew and Gentile, which is abolished since Christ's full exhibition so then take the sense of the text thus:

That first, the apostle bids the believers continue with the unbelievers or idolaters.

Secondly, adding this reason, because their fellowship is holy.

Thirdly, from an absurdity, which would else follow, and that is, else were your children unclean, but now are they holy.

An answer to that text Romans 11:16–17

In the next place let us speak to that in the 11[th chapter] of the Romans, [verses] 16–17, made use by some to prove a covenant of eternal life in the flesh, the words are these, "For if the first fruits are holy, then the lump is also holy; and if the root be holy, so are the branches; and if some of the branches are broken off, and thou being a wild olive tree, art grafted in among them, and with them partakes of the root and fatness of the olive, &c."

The usual exposition is that this root is Abraham, Isaac, and Jacob, and the branches are to be understood [as] the body of Israel that came of their loins, as the root and the branches. And so the Jews through unbelief with their generation were broken off, and so also the Gentiles with their generation and seed are brought in. This last clause, which mainly serves for their purpose, they bring in by head and shoulders, that the Gentile and his seed is brought in. What is there in that text which will countenance that clause if it be truly examined?

But let us consider this text, and see what it will afford to prove a covenant of eternal life to life, to run in the flesh of believing Gentiles; for that is what the text must prove, without the which in vain it is alleged. And for the better examining of the same, we will take for granted that by "root" is meant Abraham, and by "first-fruits" is meant Abraham, Isaac, and Jacob, which are spoken of. If so, then you must of necessity distinguish Abraham, as the apostle doth, as begetting and working Abraham, and as believing and faithful Abraham; and so thus you must understand Abraham in a two-fold covenant as hath been before cleared. Wherein he was in a double sense holy, as he was in that absolute Covenant of Grace, so considered, he was spiritually holy, and considered as in the Covenant of Works, that conditional covenant made with him, he was legally holy.

Now all the nation of the Jews, being separated by God from all other nations in and by the same covenant, are in this sense holy as Abraham was, and he was holy in a covenant of life with a spiritual holiness, so only those of the spiritual and believing seed as his branches in that sense can be said to be holy.

And the like may be said of those patriarchs who, as the first fruits, consider them in the spiritual covenant so they, as the first fruits, may be said to be spiritual and holy. So by the "lump" you must understand that seed in that covenant to be only spiritually holy, as the first-fruits were. But if you consider them in the Covenant of Works, the external, national covenant as the first fruit in that covenant were legally holy, so were that whole lump that is, the whole nation of the Jews thus holy, till that covenant was abolished and put an end to. Then this covenant entailed on the flesh of Abraham, being put an end to or abolished, it must needs be that the branches must be broken off, viz. such as only by nature or birth had an interest to that covenant, or joining only to the family.

And the distinctions of the covenants and seeds being observed, it will enlighten the soul to understand this place. We find this distinction carried on in the beginning of the chapter viz. two covenants, and two seeds, and both in the Church of Israel, such as some would call the covenanting seed. There were two seeds amongst the external covenanting seed; there was the Covenant of Works, and the Covenant of Grace, as for example. The apostle speaks of the whole body of Israel, then of a select number out of Israel, which God foreknew, and therefore brings in the case of Elijah [in] 1 Kings 19, where God had in Israel 7000 selected from the rest of the same body of Israel in the outward covenant with him. And also in the apostle's time he saith, "That there were a select number, according to the election of grace, which God had chose[n] out of Israel." Then saith he, "If by grace, then by works? If by works, then not by grace?" Where you hear the apostle clearly distinguish two seeds in Israel as two covenants, the one a conditional covenant of works, the other of grace, an absolute covenant, as in the 4th, 5th, 6th, 7th verses of that 11[th chapter] of the

Romans. So the main drift here of the apostle is to hold forth that though God did now cast off from being his Church, the carnal seed, that were only in the Covenant of Works, this covenant standing no longer in force, but growing old and vanishing way, as in Hebrews 8:13, in which covenant he chose this nation to himself. Yet, nevertheless, the apostle doth affirm that God had a remnant that were elect, that should be called that natural seed of Israel, even to the end, though for the present, the greatest part were hardened in unbelief. So that when he saith the branches are broken off, we are not to understand that such of them as related to Abraham as a father or root of believers in a covenant of grace were broken off. For then we should hold falling away from and out of a covenant of life, which would be a gross error, but branches were broken off from the root, considered in that national Covenant of Circumcision which was a covenant of works that carnal people might really be in, as you heard before. This national covenant now ceasing (as I have showed), and being put an end to by Christ, he, becoming the substance of the same covenant, and that being the partition-wall at that time, between Jews and Gentiles.

But the apostle now affirms in Galatians 5:6 and 6:16, "That circumcision availeth not anything, nor uncircumcision, but a new creature and faith and worketh by love"; therefore, all the Jews that believed not ceased to be members of God's Church. Because now Abraham is in no way considered as a father and a root in the Gospel Church, but as faithful and believing Abraham in a covenant of eternal life, therefore, unbelief now cuts off the nation of the Jews.

Why had not unbelief cut them off many hundred years before? The answer is plain, for so long as the typical Covenant of Works stood in force, Israel by being of that family or generation, whether they had faith or no, or any appearance of grace or no, were interested in that covenant and in the privileges thereof.

But now when Christ fully exhibited in the flesh, and that covenant ceasing and the Covenant of Life (now) only remaining, it becomes so that only those branches and that lump of believers, the spiritual lump only remain in the Church whether Jews or Gentiles.

So that if you will seriously mind the scope and drift of the apostle, you shall see that the lump and the branches, here intended, must needs be holy, because the first-fruits and root are holy, which is meant those of God's spiritual elect of the Jews, that he would call to the end of the world, which since is confirmed in the 28th verse. For saith the apostle, "As concerning the Gospel they are enemies for your sakes," meaning the Gentiles, "but as touching the election they are beloved for the fathers' sake." Not as if God hated these rejected Jews for the sakes of these Gentiles properly, or loved a certain number of the Jews for their fathers' sake properly.

But thus for the Gospel's sake they became enemies, that is, the Gospel promise or Covenant, having (as you have heard before) respect to all nations (Gen 12:3; 22:18 with Gal. 3:8).

Now this Gospel Covenant, being not capable to be divulged to all nations so long as this external electing love to the nation of the Jews was kept on foot in that Covenant of Circumcision, being a partition-wall. Therefore, this bond of favor and friendship, being broken in this external covenant, they came to be enemies because of the accomplishment of the promises of the Gospel to the Gentiles, that those beloved, elected of the Jews, and ten tribes even are beloved for their fathers' sake, meaning for the promise's sake, made to their fathers concerning their calling, which must needs be accomplished (Isa. 65:23), for they are the seed of the blessed of the Lord, and their offspring with them, meaning all such elected offspring as this 11[th chapter] speaks of the calling. For saith the text, "As touching the election they were beloved for the fathers' sake," so that for the promise's sake made to their Fathers, they shall in time be actually elected with an eternal electing love.

But to mind this Scripture further, it makes exceedingly against any fleshly covenant running in the fleshly line of the Gentiles because that these words in verse the 20th to the 24th do declare the Gentiles came to be Abraham's spiritual seed, and so a branch of that stock, only by faith in Christ that fat olive. "For if you are Christ's, then are ye Abraham's seed, and heirs according to promise" (Gal. 3:29). And as it said the Gentiles are graffed into this stock or root of Abraham contrary to nature, it must needs cut off such conclusion as, "That all believing Gentiles seed shall come by nature into this stock." It being not only against the whole scope and drift of this place, but against the express words which saith, the Gentiles are grafted in contrary to nature, and stand by faith, and further that unbelief broke off the Jews.

Now this would be a strange riddle (in my judgment) first to conclude, that the whole nation of the Jews were in a Covenant of Eternal Life, and yet never had faith, no not so much as visibly for the greatest part of them.

Secondly, that they were broken off, from a Covenant of Eternal Life, and why? Because of unbelief. And yet nevertheless, believing Gentiles, their unbelieving seed, in the midst of this unbelief is grafted in.

This in substance is what is drawn from this text for proving a covenant in the flesh. But let any impartially judge, how much a shame it would be, to wrest Scripture so contrary to the scope and meaning. For this chapter shows that there were two seeds, two covenants, one of grace, or the gospel, the other of works, and that men could not obtain aright to this Gospel covenant, but by virtue of election, and that merely of grace. The other Covenant of Works, and the fleshly seed in this covenant were broke off, that is, from any privilege coming from Abraham according to the flesh, that fleshly covenant being put an end to by

The Doctrine of Baptism

Christ's being come in the flesh. All unbelieving Jews upon that ground cease to be God's Church much more unbelieving Gentiles. For if unbelief broke off the Jew, be sure it will as effectually keep out the Gentile, as it is clear it doth because they stand by faith only, and are grafted in contrary nature. It is said the Jew, if he abided not in unbelief, shall be grafted again.

From all which it is plain that there is no other way now under the Gospel to come into, or stand in the house or Church of God but by faith, neither for Jew nor Gentile. And so far is the apostle free from concluding, that the Gentiles come in by nature, that he affirms the contrary, that he is grafted in contrary to nature. Plainly holding forth, that all, both Jews and Gentiles, in a state of unbelief, were excluded from those privileges.

For (as before hath been proved) the ground upon which the Covenant of Circumcision was made unto Abraham, and his seed according to the flesh, was not because he was a believer, but because Christ was to come of that line according to the flesh.

If you could find out any Gentile under the Gospel out of which the Messiah should come according to the flesh, then there were the same reason and ground that an external, typical covenant should run in his line or flesh, till the Messiah were fully exhibited.

But I hope none will be such an Anti-Christ so highly to deny Christ come in the flesh, seeing Paul saith, "Henceforth we know no man after the flesh, for saith he, We have known Christ after the flesh, but henceforth we know him so no more."[45]

That men were known, that is, approved as privileged persons in God's Church by being in that covenant entailed in the flesh of Abraham, viz. that Covenant of Circumcision; but from henceforth we know no man, no not Christ himself should be minded, as standing interessed in that covenant, he being now known, to be one receiving a more excellent ministry than the

---

[45] 2 Corinthians 5:16.

ministry of circumcision, a better covenant grounded upo[n] better promises (Heb. 8:6-7). The following words confirm this exposition, "Therefore if any man be in Christ he is a new creature, old things pass away and all things become new,"[46] compared with Galatians 6:15, "It is not circumcision availeth anything, &c; therefore, we are not now to know men according the flesh.

No not Christ as come in the flesh circumcised and by virtue of that privileged in the Church. But we are now to know him as fully exhibited, and (as before) a minister of a better covenant grounded upon better promises.

So that this 11th chapter of the Romans doth so little to serve to countenance the covenant of eternal life to run in the flesh, that it exceedingly makes against it, cuts it up by the roots, affirming no other of the Gentiles or their seed to be grafted into this stock of root, but contrary to nature, which he expounds to be by faith.

Therefore, take the whole drift and scope of that place, and you shall have two seeds, two covenants, a certain select number out of those that were in the Old Covenant, elected into the New Covenant, the rest of all the body of Israel in that Old Covenant were blinded and hardened, and never obtained an interest into the New Covenant.

And when Jesus Christ, the substance of the Old Covenant, was come, then that ceasing, and now but one covenant remaining, the covenant of God's Church, its of necessity only believers and spiritual seed now can remain in the Church. Hereupon, all the unbelieving seed of Jews and Gentiles are utterly excluded out from the Church, and Church privileges which never was so long as an old, external covenant stood in force.

An answer to that text 1 Corinthians 10:1-3

---

[46] 2 Corinthians 5:17.

The Doctrine of Baptism

The next Scripture text, brought in for defense of the covenant in the flesh, is 1 Corinthians 10:1-3, "Moreover, brethren, I would not have you ignorant, how that all our fathers were under the cloud, and all passed through the sea, and were all baptized unto Moses in the cloud and in the sea, and did all eat of that spiritual meat, and drink of that spiritual drink, for they drank of that spiritual rock that followed them, and that rock was Christ."

This is another Scripture which is made use of to prove a covenant of salvation to run in the flesh.

But beloved, the drift of the apostle here is (as it is throughout the Scripture) to give out the mystery and substance that shadows typed out to come, according to that in 2 Corinthians 3: "We are not ministers of the letter, but of the Spirit," meaning that the main thing which the apostles did hold forth in their ministry, when they had to do with types and shadows was, to set forth the substance or spirit, or heavenly things that was pointed at, and so here.

Beloved, know this, that these were all types and ceremonies here spoke of, belonging to the carnal Jew; therefore, saith the apostle, "They were all baptized unto Moses in the cloud and in the sea."[47] He doth not say they were all baptized into Christ, but unto Moses, which is the main passage I would present to you.

You must understand Moses was a solemn type, he was a savior to save them out of the land of Egypt, their present bondage, into Canaan. He was a mediator of that temporal covenant (Gal. 3:19), and in this did Moses type out Christ. The temporal covenant did type out the spiritual and heavenly covenant, and the temporal Israel did type out the spiritual Israel.

This temporal redemption of Israel out of Egypt into Canaan, typed out the spiritual redemption from sin, bondage, the world, and devil into that heavenly Canaan.

---

[47] 1 Corinthians 10:2.

The covenant that Moses was the mediator of (you heard) was the Covenant of Circumcision, which is before cleared to be a covenant of works, delivered in substance to Abraham, but after committed by writing to Moses (Acts 15:1), where the teachers did command them to be circumcised and keep the Law after the manner of Moses, compared with John 7:22: "Moses therefore gave unto you circumcision, not because it is of Moses, but of the Father." In Acts 15:1, it is said by the false teachers, "That except they were circumcised after the manner of Moses, they could not be saved." Those teachers were of the same opinion with these in our days who hold that the Covenant of Circumcision was a Covenant of Life, and therefore concluded, such persons out of it could not be saved. Their conclusion was (doubtless) answerable to the premises. For if that circumcision had been as they judged it, a Covenant of Eternal Life, then out of it, none could have been saved. Therefore, it is said in the 5th verse, "Certain of the sect of the Pharisees that believed did say, it was needful to circumcise them, and to command them to keep the Law of Moses." And in the tenth verse it is said, "Why tempt ye God to put a yoke upon the necks of the disciples, which neither our fathers nor we are able to bear," which on God's part was the promise of Canaan, with all the good things thereof, and the external privileges as protection and preservation. And on their parts, they were bound to keep the Law; therefore, you shall find that Ezra and Nehemiah, entered into an oath and a curse with the people then to keep this covenant on their part as that nation were bound to do.

And this was that covenant which the case teachers persuaded the Galatians to be a Covenant of Life, and that they could not be saved without, which covenant the Apostle Paul called the flesh in Galatians 3:2, meaning that covenant which God had established in their flesh for an everlasting covenant, as he calls it, Genesis 17:13: "This shall be my covenant in your flesh, saith the Lord, for an everlasting covenant." Therefore, saith Paul in Romans 4:1, "What shall we say that Abraham our Father as appertaining to the flesh hath found, if Abraham were justified by works?" Mark his exposition of that covenant, appertaining to the flesh to be a Covenant of Works, which in the 10th verse he clears to be circumcision in opposition to that Gospel promise, which Abraham had before he was circumcised, and so he doth all along in that chapter. Here in the 3rd chapter] of Galatians he doth set the Covenant of Grace and that of Works in opposition, the he calls the Spirit, the other flesh, which he most evidently explains in Chapters 5:1-3, where saith he, "Stand fast in that liberty which Christ hath made you free, and be not entangled again with the yoke of bondage."

Here observe again, that he calls it as Peter doth [in] Acts 15:10, "a yoke of bondage," which is evident that they were set at freedom and liberty from as that which was abolished, and they freed from as a yoke, which neither they, nor their fathers were able to bear. This appears in Galatians 5:1-3: "Behold, I, Paul, say to you, if ye be circumcised, Christ shall profit you nothing:" Nay, in v. 3, "For I testify to everyone that is circumcised, that he is a debtor to do the whole Law," and ver[se] 4, he sets it in opposition to the Covenant of Grace, and this is explained more in Galatians chapter 6, verses 12-13.

Now all this considered, you may clearly see the Covenant of Circumcision made to Abraham and his seed in their generation, that he would give them Canaan with the blessings thereof, and in that sense, be their God to protect, preserve, and externally to privilege them with the means of grace, and tenders of the Gospel, and the external blessings of Canaan, upon condition they would be circumcised and keep the Law.

All these things are typical, this deliverance out of Egypt, typing out the deliverance out of Hell. That temporal Israel after the flesh, that were redeemed out of Egypt, typed out the spiritual Israel that were redeemed out of the spiritual bondage.

And (as before hath been said) Moses then was a temporal redeemer, mediator, or savior, typed out Christ, the spiritual mediator and savior. Therefore, in 1 Corinthians 10:6, the apostle tells us these were our figures or types.

So this being premised, we have the sense of the text here plain, that as the spiritual disciple or Israelite, when he believes and confesses his faith, thereby showing his interest in Jesus Christ, is baptized into Christ Jesus, the mediator of that covenant, which he is in by faith.

So the temporal Israel by birth, or being bought with money, or cohabitation in that family of Israel, coming to have a right to the Covenant of Circumcision, whereof Moses was the mediator, they were likewise baptized unto Moses, as our baptism is a confirmation to the spiritual Israel of their spiritual deliverance by Jesus their mediator from death and condemnation to eternal life.

And whereas the apostle calls that meat spiritual meat, and that drink, spiritual drink, he here speaks figuratively, as before affirmed. Not that the Manna eaten by the whole nation of Israel, was in itself spiritual, but it was a figure of the spiritual bread. Therefore, Christ saith to the Jews in John 6:32–33: "Verily, verily, I say unto you, Moses gave you not that bread from heaven, but my Father giveth you the true bread from heaven." Observe that word, "giveth," not "did give," but "giveth" for the bread of God is that which cometh down from heaven, and "giveth" life to the world.

And therefore, saith he, "My Father giveth you the true bread from heaven," that is, the substance of that shadow, and so that rock was Christ, meaning a figure, or type of Christ.

What is all this, beloved, to the proving of a Covenant of Life, running in the flesh, either then, or now, to the Gentiles under the Gospel, seeing it is clear, that all these ordinances (as the apostle calls them [in] Hebrews 9, carnal ordinances) did type out, or figure out, spiritual and substantial things? For their

The Doctrine of Baptism

sacrifices for sin, typed out Christ, but they were not Christ, and their typical remissions, which they had by their sacrifice, that remission, I say, which the whole body of Israel had by offering up their sin-offering can be understood to be no other but typical.

A man might be under that typical remission, and yet be under the wrath of God and be damned, and a poor Gentile, at the utmost part of the earth, believing as Rahab did in Canaan, as truly justified, though he had none of this typical remission, and none of these before mentioned figures, so that we conclude the whole nation of the Jews had not a Covenant of Eternal Life in the flesh made unto them, though they had a temporal, typical covenant as I have all along called it. That is, consisting of such laws and privileges that had not Christ in them, but did point at him to come. Therefore, they are called in Hebrews 9 patterns of heavenly things, but not the very things themselves. They are called by the apostle, "beggarly elements or rudiments of the world, or a schoolmaster to lead to Christ." The Jews' literal obedience to the Law, typing out the obedience to faith (Deut. 30:12-14 with Rom. 10 from v. 6 to the 10th ver[se]).

Now beloved, the literal obedience in itself performed by the carnal Jew, though it figured out the substantial obedience, viz. faith in Christ, though the rest in Canaan, typed out the spiritual rest in Christ, yet I hope no man will be so absurd, but he will confess that this literal obedience, it was not the spiritual obedience, and that this rest in Canaan it was but a shadow of that rest in Christ, not the very rest itself.

But some may say so of baptism, and the Supper, that these are the signs of inward and spiritual things, but it doth not follow, that these are the spiritual things.

Beloved, observe warily, for here lies the ground of this great mistake, the want of distinguishing between these figures that type out Christ to come, and these sacramental signs that do confirm and ratify his being already come.

Those typical signs and figures, then, which typed out Christ to come, did properly belong to that typical seed, the body of Israel, that typed out the spiritual seed to come.

But now these signs, I say, these sacramental signs that are instituted since Christ came, for the confirming he is come, these belong only to the spiritual seed, in whom Christ is come already dwelling in their hearts by faith.

Therefore as Christ is a spiritual and substantial mediator of a substantial and spiritual covenant, so these spiritual administrations of the spiritual covenant belong only to such as are in Christ, and this new covenant by faith, and that have Christ dwelling in them, as hath been before in the former part of my discourse, manifested.

In the New Testament, faith and repentance are required of them that are to be baptized, "Here is water; what letteth? If thou believest with all thy heart, it is lawful" (Acts 8:38), implying it was unlawful to baptize any that did not believe with all their heart at least in profession. And so when Christ dispenseth the Supper, he commands it to be received by his disciples (Matt. 26). He saith to his disciples, "Take eat," and he said to his disciples, "Drink ye all of this, "and Paul saith, "Examine yourselves and so eat of this bread, and drink of this cup."[48]

If you will not shut your eyes against the light, there is nothing more plain than this, that those administrations under the Old Covenant did not require such qualifications as are essentially requisite to be found in the persons that must partake of these substantial signs of the New Covenant.

As for circumcision, it was not necessary for all that were circumcised to believe and repent, or to have faith in Christ, or to be converted, and made disciples by preaching as necessary qualifications to partake of the ordinances. But the institution in Genesis 17:13 saith, "All born in thy house, or bought with thy money," though never so ignorant, carnal, or have never so

---

[48] 1 Corinthians 11:28.

The Doctrine of Baptism

wicked parents or parentage, yet such ought to be circumcised, this institution running upon that family.

But baptism is a confirmation of our regeneration already wrought in us, and our new birth, and our union with Jesus Christ by faith, and therefore belongs only to them where this regeneration is, to them that are born again of water and of the Spirit. And so the Passover was to be partaken of by the carnal Israelite after the flesh, viz. the captive, the slave bought with money, heathen, black moor, or of the Canaanites, but the Lord's Supper only belongs to disciples able to discern the Lord's body by faith, without the which they bring judgment upon themselves, and make themselves guilty of the body and blood of the Lord, except they are able to examine themselves, "Let a man examine himself, and so let him eat of the bread, and drink of that cup." So that which the apostle drives at in this chapter is this, principally, that the temporal Israel who were the Church of God then privileged in that temporal covenant upon their falls and sins, were by God visited and corrected, to show to all the world that he would not countenance sin without sad reproof. Likewise, he concludes in this also the Gospel-Church professing the Covenant of Grace, and enjoying the privileges thereof, they should not escape if they turn aside from God, and sin against him without checks, reproofs and sad admonitions from him. Here lies the scope, all that might such caution be given to Gospel churches because they were in a Covenant of Grace only by a visible profession, and therefore may possibly receive the greater danger by sin if their profession should not be right and saving.

Object. But some may object, "That there were some precious saints then in the Old Testament, and do you think that they did not perform the ordinances with spiritual hearts?"

Answ. No question such did, as it is said of Abel, "By faith he offered a more excellent sacrifice than Cain."

Duties performed from faith with an eye to Christ were then acceptable, when so performed, though ceremoniously, and such duties relating merely to the Covenant of Works.

Faith made not Israelites capable of performing the ceremonies of the Law
Only I would have you observe, that the carnal Israelite was without faith capable to perform every ceremonial law required by the Old Covenant according to the express tenor thereof, as truly as the believer.

So in no wise can it be said of the duties relating to the New Covenant, either then, or now as repentance, spiritual prayer, thanksgiving, and divers other duties perpetually at all times, and universal to all saints. I deny that the carnal Jews were capable of the true performance of these; I mean to answer the rules or institutions given. For if you look to the catechism in the Common Prayer Book, you shall find that it was a maxim, received by all that own that liturgy, that no less than a profession of faith and repentance was required of them that were baptized.[49]

Object. But may some say, "Did not some bring their friends to Christ to be healed, and Christ, seeing the faith of those which brought them healed them? And if they believed for others, to the healing of their bodies, why not also then for the saving of their souls?"

Answ. This is directly the Papists' argument, with which some do close rather than part with their idol. But to speak to this more particularly, there is nothing more plain than that God did give gifts of healing to many as that the faith of one

---

[49] The catechism to which Patient refers precedes the rite of confirmation in the 1604 Book of Common Prayer, also known as the "Hampton Court Book." The specific question and answer in the said catechism to which he alludes is: "Question: What is required of persons to be baptized? Answer: Repentance, whereby they forsake sin: and faith, whereby they steadfastly believe the promises of God, made to them in that sacrament."

contributed to the healing of the body of another, as their servants and children, as in the case of the centurion in Matthew 8, the 7th, 8th, 9th verses, and Jarius, the ruler over the synagogue.

But this is no way to prove that one man should come to have union with Christ, and so to have justification and eternal life by the faith of another.

For in this case the prophet saith, "The just shall live by faith" (Hab. 2:4; Rom. 1:17). And he that believes not is condemned already, that is, every individual, he that believes not, shall be condemned, and he that believeth shall be saved. But some do bring in that text in the 7[th chapter] of the Hebrews, that Levi paid tithes in Abraham; therefore, why should not souls believe and repent in their believing parents as well as Levi paid tithes in his believing father, Abraham?

It seems to me that this act of Abraham was performed as a public person in his paying tithes to Melchizedek, herein representing his posterity; but not so in all the rest of his acts. It doth not follow that he believed and repented for all his posterity; for this were a notable ground indeed for Papists' implicit faith.[50]

We know that Adam in his fall, did act sin as a public person in which all mankind are said to sin, Romans 5. But it doth not follow that all the future acts that Adam committed he did perform as a public person. If all the posterity of a believing person so many generations to come, as Levi from Abraham, did believe and repent in their believing parents, then there is no ground to oppose, that all the world at this day are believers

---

[30] What Patient considers to be the Roman Catholic concept of "implicit faith" is really what the Roman Church teaches as "unformed faith," which is the ability to believe in God's existence and his justice infused into the infant through the sacrament of baptism. "Implicit faith," on the other hand, refers to the faith of one who is unlearned, believing simply without understanding, as opposed to "explicit faith," which characterizes that of the Christian who understands what he/she believes and why. The first to make this distinction between "implicit" and "explicit" faith was Peter Lombard (1096-1160). See Philipp W. Rosemann, *Peter Lombard* (Oxford: Oxford University Press, 2004).

because they were all in the line of believing Noah, he being the father from whence all the world did proceed that are now living this day.

And again observe, that if the Covenant of Life belongs to all believers' seed, then we need not want for church members because all the world are the children and offspring of believing Noah, and this argument carries the right of covenant to all the world, being children of a believer, viz. Noah.

An answer to that text Matthew 19:13

Further, some bring that in Matthew 19:13: "There were brought unto him little children that he should put his hand upon them and pray, and the disciples rebuked them, and Jesus said, Suffer little children and forbid them not to come to me, for of such is the kingdom of God; and he laid his hands on them and departed."

In Mark 10:13 thus: "And they brought young children to him, that he should touch them, and his disciples rebuked them that brought them, but when Jesus saw it, he was much displeased, and said unto them, Suffer the little children to come unto me and forbid them not, for of such is the kingdom of God; verily I say unto you, whosoever shall not receive the Kingdom of God as a little child, shall not enter therein."

From hence would some maintain in a Covenant of Eternal Life in the flesh, for that end they bring this text, but let us examine what the meaning of it may be.

First, whose children they were, that were brought to Christ doth not appear, it's probable they were the seed of Abraham, but what their mediate parents, whether believers or wicked persons doth not appear certainly, but by the former discourse in the chapter, it should seem they might be wicked and ungodly persons; for there were such mentioned before that tempted Christ, and asked him questions.

The Doctrine of Baptism

The next thing is, for what did they bring these children unto Christ? Most certain not to baptize them because Christ, it is said, baptized not, but the disciples (John 4:2). What then were they brought to Christ for? One evangelist saith, "He took them in his arms and blessed them." Another saith, "He laid his hands on them and prayed."

All which considered (in my judgment) it doth probably appear, they were brought to him to be healed of some disease, it being usual in those days that by prayer and laying on of hands, they did heal the sick.

But the main expression in the text to be noted is this, "That of such are the Kingdom of God."

From these words some gather that all the children of believing parents do belong to the kingdom of God, and if to the Kingdom of God, then to all the privileges of that kingdom.

But (as you have heard) it will be very doubtful whether these children had any believing parents to the fifth or sixth degree, for "of such is the Kingdom of God," saith the text, the which we must understand thus: That all the children of born of the body of believers, and that when little ones in arms do belong to the Kingdom of God, if you will make this text to countenance the error of the covenant in the flesh, the which is erroneous, as appears, in that the greatest number of believers' children never belonged in that sense to the Kingdom of God. Adam had a Cain as well as an Abel, Noah had a Ham as well as a Shem, Abraham had an Ishmael as well as an Isaac, Isaac had an Esau as well as a Jacob. And so I might mention all the scriptures, wherein in like manner God doth as well bring forth generation of the wicked out of the godly, and the generation of the elect, out of the line of the wicked, indefinitely.

But if by "Kingdom of God" be meant that condition or state that men are interested in, by virtue of a covenant of eternal life, and that believers' children should by birth and generation belong to it, then this fully crosseth that doctrine of Christ to Nicodemus (John 3:5), as was formerly spoken to.

Object. But some may say, "It is possible that such a little child may believe, because in Matthew 18, 3rd, 4th, 5th, 6th verses, it is said, 'We should not offend such little ones that believe.'"

If you grant that some children, when little do believe, and therefore belong to the Kingdom of God, to that I assent, let them be whose children they will, whether of believers or infidels.

If they believe they are in Christ, and so interested in the Kingdom of God.

But what makes this for the covenant in the flesh of carnal, unbelieving seed?

Again, if by "Kingdom of God," should be understood the Jewish state or church, and children here understood for children of that Jewish nation, then, in that sense, it is true that all children born in the Jewish church by virtue of their birth in that family or nation belonged as members to that national church, being interested in the Covenant of Circumcision, which was the national covenant, and the privileges of the same, and were, by natural birth, interested therein.

Answ. But the true and proper meaning of the text appears plain to be here in Mark 10:13–15, compared together, for when he had in the 14th verse said, "Of such belongeth the Kingdom of God" in verse the 15th, he presently saith, "Verily I say unto you, whosoever receivieth not the kingdom of God as a little child shall not enter therein." This I say interprets these words before, "Of such is the kingdom of God," that is, of such like in grace, as these by nature, such souls that are by God's grace, subdued and brought into a child-like frame of spirit, they only are such as are of the Kingdom of God, as for example.

The Doctrine of Baptism

When the disciples reasoned who should be greatest among them, Christ set a little child as a pattern of humility, innocency, and harmlessness.

And also saith the apostle, "Be you children in malice, and old men in understanding" (1 Cor. 14). And saith Peter, "As newborn babes, desire the sincere milk of the word, that ye might grow thereby" (1 Pet. 2:2).

And so as there is a parity held forth between a child in nature, and a child in grace, as the natural begetting, the spiritual begetting, alluding to that, there is the natural birth and the spiritual birth held forth, by that sucking of the mother's breast, and by sucking of the breast of God's word.

A little babe we know in nature will trust his parents, so the new born babe will trust in Christ. If the natural babe want anything, it will go to its parents, and ask them for it, so must a newborn babe make his request known to God in all his wants. If anything hurt a babe, he will cry, and make his complaint to his father. So the child of God, if any straight oppresseth him, he cries to God his Father. The natural child will imitate his father and his brethren, so the newborn imitates God the Father and Christ, the rest (as it were) of his brethren. The newborn babe, when young, a little will content it, so should the newborn babe in grace be in all conditions and states content.

And this I understand to be the proper meaning of this place, "Of such is the Kingdom of God," that is, of such souls that are spiritually qualified by God's grace, answerable to little children in nature (Matt. 18:1-6), of such godly newborn heavenly babes, is the Kingdom of God.

And this exposition agrees with the right scope of the place, and the true analogy of faith.

And therefore I would have you seriously to consider that this Covenant of Grace in the flesh, the whole word of the Lord disclaims it, and will give no countenance to any such notion, destructive in its consequence, to the truth of God (as you have heard before).

Object. But some may object and say, "But this which you call a Covenant of Works, consisting of temporal promises, and also laws and statutes, you are not to understand that to be a distinct covenant from the Covenant of Eternal Life, but a form of administration, that the Covenant of Grace was then administered in. And the carnal children were not then interessed in the main privileges of the covenant as adoption and justification, but the outward promises and privileges only made to their fathers."

Answ. I know this objection some do bring, which if it be well weighed, is inconsistent with their own arguments.

For if this objection be true, then was there no covenant made with Abraham's seed, but only an administration of a covenant. And therefore ill do they affirm that the covenant was made to them; therefore, the administration. But this doubtless is false, and this objection (as I said) is false and groundless as appears by several express testimonies in Scripture which doth evidently prove two distinct covenants, as for example.

Saith God in Genesis chapter 17 and verse 7: "And I will establish my covenant between me and thee, and thy seed after thee in their generations for an everlasting covenant, to be a God to thee, and to thy seed after thee."

Where observe, that the Lord doth not say that he will establish an administration of the covenant, with his seed in their generations, but his covenant, and Abraham and his seed, must keep his covenant. In verse the 13th, "this my covenant shall be in your flesh, for an everlasting covenant," not "this administration of my covenant shall be in your flesh, and in Hebrews the 8[th chapter] verses 6–9, "But now hath he obtained a more excellent ministry by how much also he is the mediator of a better covenant which he established upon better promises."

The Doctrine of Baptism

Mark (as I have before showed at large) here were two covenants, the one upon better promises, the other upon worse promises, which must needs be understood temporal blessings, and deliverances and privileges. Therefore, he saith, "they serve unto the example and shadow of heavenly things," and in verse the seventh, "if that first testament had been faultless, there should have no place sought for the second." And in the ninth verse he saith that "the old covenant they continued not in; therefore God regarded them not; and in verse the 12th in that he saith, "a new covenant he hath made the first old." Now that which decayeth, and waxeth old, is ready to vanish away, which scriptures do evidence as clear as the sun at noon day, that there was a real covenant made with the Jews, made before with Abraham, but committed to the Church in writing by Moses, when he led them out of Egypt, and this covenant they brake, said Jeremiah 31:32. And here the apostle saith, "they continued not in it," and the last verse saith, it was made old, and therefore vanishing away. And in Hebrews 9, there the apostle calls this old covenant that contained in it shadows and patterns of heavenly things, the first Testament wherein the apostle in verse 17 and forwards, doth show there were two testaments, the one confirmed by the blood of bulls, the other confirmed by the blood of Christ. And if this were not true, then most falsely do such affirm the covenant was made with Abraham's seed; therefore, the privileges, if Abraham lineally had no covenant made with them, but only an external and outward administration and privilege, &c.

Upon the ground there was no national covenant at all made with Israel, but only an outward administration, and that being granted to be ceremonial, except you can prove another ceremonial administration as carnal, as that administration was, now in force, there is not the like ground why carnal and unbelieving children should have any share in it.

THOMAS PATIENT

An exposition of that text Galatians 4:21
But that there were two covenants is most evident as appears in the New Testament, as I have formerly at large endeavored to make good, only I shall add that in Galatians 4:21, and forward, where saith the apostle, "Tell me, ye that would be under the Law, do you not hear the Law, for it is written, That Abraham had two sons, the one by a bond-maid, the other by a free-woman, but he who was of the bond-woman was born after the flesh, but he of the free-woman was by promise, which things are an allegory, that is, by these things other things are meant."

For these are the two covenants, the one from Mount Sinai, which gendereth to bondage, which is Hagar; for this Hagar is Mount Sinai in Arabia, and answereth to Jerusalem that now is, and is in bondage with her children, but Jerusalem, which is above, is free, which is the mother of us all.

Now we, brethren, as Isaac was, are children of the promise, but as then, he that was born after the flesh persecuted him that was born after the Spirit; so it is now, notwithstanding, cast out the bond-woman and her son; for the son of the bond-woman shall not be heir with the son of the free-woman. So then, brethren, we are not children of the bond-woman, but of the free." And in the next chapter he saith, "Stand fast therefore in the liberty wherewith Christ hath made you free, and be not entangled again, with the yoke of bondage, which he afterwards explains to be the Covenant of Circumcision" (Gal. 5:1–3).

But to speak something of this text, Abraham here by the apostle is understood to represent God by way of type and figure, as it were, his two women Sarah and Hagar, the two covenants of God; the two sons, Ishmael and Isaac, represents (as the text hints) the two seeds in these two covenants of God. Now Sarah, the free-woman, represents the Covenant of Grace, and Hagar the Covenant of Works. Both these women continued in Abraham's house together for a time, the first child he begat by the strength of nature, without faith in a promise of a bond-woman. The other he begat by faith in a promise without strength of nature, of a free-woman; and the free-woman continued in Abraham's house with the bond-woman and her son without any scruple till Isaac was born and weaned. And when the son of the bond-woman persecuted Isaac, the free-woman testifies against the bond-woman and her son, and will have them no longer to abide in the house with her son. Abraham likewise had first the free-woman, and the last the bond-woman. The free-woman was sometime barren in Abraham's house, but the bond-woman was fruitful.

Now the mystery that the apostle hints to be held forth in this history is clear, from which he speaks in this 4th [chapter] of the Galatians which must be this.

That God in like manner first made a Covenant of Grace, even as Abraham first had a free-woman, which covenant (in a great measure) was barren, bringing forth no seed, or else totally barren as Sarah was, in respect of that substantial seed, Christ Jesus, which Isaac typed forth, as soon as God had made this covenant, he in the same house or Church hath also a Hagar, that is a covenant of works in which God hath abundance of seed, becoming his by strength of nature, without faith in a promise, and the Covenant of Grace as Sarah (in a sense) becomes barren. All which time the Covenant of Grace and Covenant of Works both agree very well to be in God's house together, but at the last, as the free-woman brought forth Isaac, so the Covenant of Grace brings forth Christ Jesus without strength of nature, by faith in a promise as in Matthew 1:21, Luke 1:35, and when this substantial seed is come, then the Covenant of Grace and Works remain in God's Church together, but afterwards when Christ the true Isaac was (as it were) weaned, that is, come to maturity so as to appear, that he was now in the office of the ministry, the scribes and Pharisees with the high priests, all the sons of Hagar, the Old Covenant, persecuted Christ, and those in him.

Whereupon the free-woman, or rather the free Covenant of Grace, doth testify that a Covenant of Works, with her seed, shall no longer remain with her in the Church of God.

But now the free covenant and her sons, that is, the Covenant of Grace only, and her children born by faith in a promise, only must for a time forward remain in the house of God.

So that now rejoice thou barren that barest not, the Covenant of Grace becomes fruitful, having seed in all nations, therefore, the apostle saith, the Jerusalem which is above, which is free, is the mother of us all, and those "us" or "we," that were members of the primitive church, were born from above by faith in a promise.

Therefore, it is plain from hence, that there were no carnal babes in that church. But when Christ, the true seed of the covenant, was persecuted by the Jews, which were the children of the Covenant of Works, the Gospel doth plentifully testify the abolishing the Covenant of Works, and the casting forth of those bond-children out of God's Church: "But when the Jews saw the multitude they were filled with envy, and spake against those things which were spoken by Paul, contradicting and blaspheming. Then Paul and Barnabas waxed bold and said, it was necessary that the word of God should first have been spoken to you, but seeing ye put it far from you, and judge yourselves unworthy of everlasting life, lo, we turn to the Gentiles; for so hath the Lord commanded us," (Acts 13:45–46). And as it appears in the 11th chapter of the Romans, and as that 4th chapter of Galatians in express words saith in the 25th verse, "This Hagar is meant Mount Sinai in Arabia, and answereth to Jerusalem that now is, and is in the bondage with her children." This being so clear that the bond-woman, and her son, that is to say, the Covenant of Works, and all those related to Abraham only in a covenant of works, are cast out of the house of God.

The Doctrine of Baptism

How opposite then is their opinion to the truth, that still would have a fleshly generation to be in the house of God with their children.

But seeing the natural branches that truly were descended of the line of faithful Abraham might not have the honor, how much less the unbelieving seed of the Gentiles that are wild by nature.

Thus you see in brief this objection is answered, and that there is no ground for children's baptism, but an imagination, through thick darkness, upon the minds of people. They, setting up this idol in their hearts, God hath answered them accordingly as the prophet speaks in Ezekiel 14, 2nd, 3rd, 4th, 5th verses: "And the word of the Lord came unto me, saying, Son of man, these men have set up their idols in their heart, and put their stumbling block of their iniquity before their face, should I be inquired of at all by them? Therefore, speak unto them, thus saith the Lord, Every man of the house of Israel, that setteth up his idols in his heart, and putteth the stumbling block of his iniquity before his face, and cometh to the prophet, I the Lord will answer him that cometh according to the multitude of his idols that I may take the house of Israel in their own heart, because they are all estranged from me through their idols."

Where you see, that when souls set up an idol in their heart, God doth answer them according to their idol, as he hath in this case suffering blind blindness and uncertainty of judgment to befall them.

For such as defend children's baptism, and the ablest I have met with, do grant they have no command or example in the New Testament for their practice, but ground the same on a consequence, which you have heard evidently proved, is drawn from an error. For to affirm or maintain, that the Covenant of Eternal Life, is made with believers' carnal seed, is a dangerous error, and therefore the consequence must needs be as false and rotten as the error from whence it is drawn, then judge you what a pitiful consequence that must be.

Take the whole result thus, children's baptism, hath no ground from the Word of God, either command or example for it, but a consequence (as before) so that it is merely a tradition of men, setting up in the place and room of the commands of God, to wit, baptizing of believers. This groundless tradition, which makes void the commandment of God, even as the wicked Jews did in Mark 7:7: "Howbeit in vain saith the Lord they worship me, teaching for doctrines the commandments of men," and in verse 9: "He said unto them, Full well you reject or frustrate the commandments of God, that you may keep your own traditions," and in verse 13: "Make the word of God of none effect through your traditions which you have delivered, and many such things do you."

Now beloved, this is the very sin of such as defend this tradition, they thereby make void and frustrate the commandment of God. See where Christ saith, "Repent and be baptized every one of you," that is, everyone that repents. And saith, Ananias to Paul, "Arise now, why tarriest thou, and be baptized for the washing away of thy sins." Peter to Cornelius his family, he there, in Acts 10:48, commands them to be baptized in the name of the Lord Jesus. Those and many more standing commands of the New Testament that belong to believers and penitent persons are frustrate and made void by christening children.

Thus, poor souls are nursed up in a habit of disrespect and disobedience to these commandments, because this invention takes the place and room of the same.

Do but consider how dangerous a sin this practice is, it is setting up a superstitious invention in the room of God's command in his worship.

Now God and his commandments must not be separated; for a soul that rightly sets up God's commandments sets up and

The Doctrine of Baptism

exalts God, and to set up any worship in the room of what is commanded of God, is in effect to set up a false God.

Do but see what sad witnesses God hath given from heaven against this sin in Leviticus 10:1-2, where Nadab and Abihu offered strange fire to God, as the text saith, which he commanded not, for which God burned them with fire from heaven; the Lord doth not say which he had forbidden, but which he commanded not. Many souls ask where God hath forbid this practice of children's baptism; therefore, I would prove by these scriptures that things or persons in the worship of God in room of what God commands are abominable to God. Hear how God doth threaten a people for this sin in Jeremiah 9:13-15: "And the Lord said, Because they had forsaken my Law which I had set before them, and have not obeyed my voice, nor walked therein, but have walked after the imagination of their own hearts." Therefore he saith in verse 15: "He will give them to feed on wormwood, and give them water of gall to drink, and will consume them." Now this is the very case of such as set this tradition; they forsake the law of believers' baptism set before them, and have never obeyed his voice nor walked therein; but have walked in children's sprinkling, which the imagination of their own hearts have devised. This text is very much applicable to such souls: the like evil wicked Saul is said to do, (1 Sam. 13, 12th, 13th verses), for which God rends the kingdom from him. And in Jeremiah 8:9: "The wisemen are dismayed and ashamed, lo, they have rejected the word of the Lord, and what wisdom is in them? Therefore, will I give their wives to others, and their fields to them that shall inherit them." And so in Jeremiah 7:31: "They have built the high places of Tophet, which is in the valley of the Son of Hinnom, to burn their sons and daughters in the fire, which I commanded them not, neither came it in my heart": upon which he threatens destruction upon them.

And you see how God made a breach upon Uzzah for touching the Ark, God not commanding him, or giving him rule for such practice. God, having given a command to the priests only to do that work, but not to him: so God hath given a command and example to baptize believers only, and not children. Therefore, it is the sin of Uzzah, and likewise the sin of King Uzziah (2 Chron. 26:14-15), where you see the said judgment of God upon Uzziah for doing that in the worship of God, which God had not commanded. In the room or stead of what he had commanded, God struck him with leprosy, and that in his forehead, and the hand of God prosecuted him, as an admonition to persons that now dare adventure upon the like sinful practices, to offer anything to God as religious worship, which he hath not commanded instead of what he hath commanded. The Lord in his case sets out himself to be a jealous God that will visit the sins of the father upon the children to the third and fourth generation of such as make to themselves any graven image, that is, any form by which we will worship God; be sure it is of God's own making, for we must not make it to ourselves. The Lord doth call in Scripture such like worship, which men do in the room of God's commanded worship, the worship of devils. I shall give you one instance for this in Scripture, as in Psalm 106:35-36, "and they served their idols which were a snare unto them, yea they sacrificed their sons and their daughters unto devils," and the next verse expounding himself, it is said, "they offered them unto the idols of Canaan.

And in like manner, do not men bring their sons and their daughters in this case, and offer them to this invention of sprinkling.

You have for baptizing of believers the commandment of Christ, and testimony of the infallible pen-men, and all men in the world owning the scriptures to be the Word of God, to be of the Lord's own institution, but this practice of children's sprinkling, God hath raised up in all ages some that have professed religion to witness against it, and a great part of those that have the power of godliness do renounce it as a sinful practice, and that upon substantial grounds. And me thinks when you consider that your children's sprinkling hath no command or example in the Gospel to confirm it, and only such a consequence that flows from error.

I hope such as fear God will take heed how they harden their hearts in the practice of so heinous a sin, and in the neglect of so solemn a duty as the ordinance of dipping believers in the name of the Father, Son, and Holy Ghost. Is there any man able to declare from Scripture that ever any solemn ordinance of standing use in the church of the New Testament had for its institution any less than a command of God, and a promise of blessing to the faithful performance of the same. But there is for children's baptism neither command to institute, nor any promise to bless, but rather indeed, the performers of that worship may respect a curse, and not a blessing in the performance of the same, as you have it in Psalm 99:8: "Thou answerest them O Lord our God, thou art a God that forgavest them, though thou tookest vengeance of their inventions" (with Ps. 106:29). Thus, they provoked him to anger with their inventions, and the plague broke in upon them, as it did in the 2 Chronicles 26:19-21:

> Then Uzziah was wroth, and had a censor in his hand to burn incense, and while he was wroth with the priests, the leprosy rose up in his forehead before the priests in the House of the Lord from besides the incense altar, and Azariah the Chief Priest, and all the rest of the priests looked upon him, and behold, he was leprous in his forehead, and they thrust him out from thence, yea himself hastened to go out because the Lord had smitten him. And Uzziah the King was a leper to the day of his death, and dwelt in a several house, for he was cut off from the House of the Lord.

THOMAS PATIENT

Thus you see the sad curse of God executed against such like inventions in the service of God that men set up in the room of God's commands, thereby jostling out his commands, as Scripture saith.

This is for a man to set up his posts by God's posts, and in a sense, setting up himself in the place and room of God, and flows from abundance of pride. As here it is said of King Uzziah, preceding this his sin, his heart was lifted up to his own destruction.

Not most certain it is, that man, Moses, was faithful in all God's house as a servant in giving the Church then, exact and perfect rules, how they should serve God, unto which they must not add and from which they must not detract, nor take away, (Deut. 4:2), so Christ is every way as faithful over his house as Lord (Heb. 3, 4, 5, 6), and rightly to this purpose is applied that in Colossians 2:8 and with [verses] 20, 21, 22.

For men to embrace any worship to their God that they have not a rule for, it is in that chapter condemned as will-worship, and traditions of men; and warily consider that it fosters men in a sinful neglect of that holy and solemn ordinance of dipping believers.

Do not all our Protestant authors in all their disputations against the Papists, defend that faith and repentance precede baptism, thereby confuting the Papists that baptism is not to convey grace where it is not, but to confirm grace, and strengthen it were it is? And in that catechism embraced generally by all Protestants in the common liturgy of England,[51] this question being demanded, "What is required of them that are to be baptized?" The answer is, "faith and repentance,"[52] which doth plainly manifest, that it was the judgment of those that were Protestants, owning that liturgy, that none ought to

---

[51] Book of Common Prayer.

[52] The answer stated in the Catechism is: "Repentance, whereby they forsake sin: and faith, whereby they steadfastly believe the promises of God, made them in that sacrament."

be baptized, but such as repent and believe. Not only so, but that do confess faith and repentance, because in baptism there is, as Peter saith, "The answer of a good conscience" (1 Pet. 3:19). Compare this with Philip and the Eunuch, Acts 8:38: "If thou believest that with all thy heart thou mayest." Saith the Eunuch, "I believe that Jesus Christ is the Son of God." So in Acts 19 it is said, "They came to the Apostle confessing their deeds."

Now consider that this doctrine in all those times was defended, that faith and repentance, must needs precede baptism. Why? Because they concluded it a seal of the New Covenant, and therefore where persons were not in a covenant by faith, did in apposition to the Papists defend, they had no interest in baptism.

Now let any soul that is not blinded with the subtly of Satan, and by means of the stumbling block of iniquity, set up in his own heart, as saith the Lord in Ezekiel 14:4. Let such I say judge how cross to this doctrine they do practice that do baptize visible, graceless and Christless children, so far as any man is able to judge.

Object.: But some will say, "I grant this, baptizing of children is a mere tradition, and that not to be practiced by Christians, and I do believe in the primitive time, believers only had this obedience dispensed upon them. But I do conceive (saith the soul) I have received the baptism of the Holy Ghost; therefore, I need not that ordinance of baptism by water, and the rather, because I think that was John's baptism, and the baptism of the Holy Ghost being come, hath put an end to that baptism of water."

Answer: Then you deny in judgement any ordinance of baptism at all to stand in force, which is be sure an upstart opinion, exceeding cross to the doctrine of Christ in his Gospel; but let me as warily as I can answer this question.

First, you do think it was John's baptism. It is true that John baptized, or dipped in water, those that came to him, confessing their sins, and professing faith in him, that should come after him.

But though it is true, John's baptism, in this respect, pointing out Christ to come, is done always, yet it is as true that the Lord hath afresh, since his death and resurrection, entitled this ordinance of dipping believers into Christ already come and fully exhibited in the flesh (Matt. 28:19-20 with Mark 16:16). And Peter after the Holy Ghost was, in that extraordinary manner, powered down upon him according to John's prophecy, to wit, with cloven fiery tongues, he doth after this, by the direction of the infallible Spirit, command all his converts that were pricked in the heart (Acts 2:38), to repent and be baptized every one of them for the remission of sins, and they should receive the gift of the Holy Ghost.

Where you may see, that this was baptism of water, that he commanded all that repent to submit to, because the Holy Ghost, as those extraordinary gifts was to follow, to wit, those gifts that Joel prophesied of.[53] And so in Acts 10, when Cornelius and his house had heard the Word of God, the Holy Ghost fell upon them, and as an effect thereof, they spake with new tongues, and magnified God, "And then saith Peter to them of the circumcision, How should we forbid water that these should not be baptized which have received the Holy Spirit as we all see?" So that this great apostle was so far from this opinion, that he urgeth the contrary, that because they had received the Holy Ghost, and that in the extraordinary gifts thereof, which John foretold, Christ should baptize them with, saith he, "How shall we forbid water," plainly holding forth, that it is baptism by water that he here is speaking of, and in which verse 48, he commanded them to be baptized in the name of the Lord Jesus, because they received the Holy Ghost. Therefore, they must not be denied that ordinance of baptism of water, clearly holding forth that the enjoying the Holy Ghost was

---

[53] Joel 2:28-32.

The Doctrine of Baptism

so far from being an argument why souls should not be baptized with water, that is an argument that they ought be baptized more especially, and this appears in Paul after his conversion, which I understand, was wrought by Christ immediately.

For saith he to Ananias, "Behold he is a chosen vessel to me, for he now prayeth;"[54] therefore, say I he was now converted as to the inward work of faith, changing his heart. "But when Ananias came to him, he laid his hands upon him: and there were two effects of this, his laying on of his hands he received his sight, and was filled with the Holy Ghost and he arose forthwith and was baptized,"[55] that is to say, after he was filled with the Holy Ghost, he arose and was baptized in water (Acts 9:17-18 compared with Acts 22:16). When Paul had received the Holy Ghost, Ananias saith, "And now Paul, why tarriest thou? Arise and be baptized, for the washing away of thy sins, calling upon the name of the Lord."

Observe that Ananias had an immediate extraordinary commission from Christ by vision to come with the message to Paul, and Christ in a vision bids Paul go to Ananias and he should tell him what he should do, and Ananias according to that commission of Christ upon his being filled with the Holy Ghost, commands him to be baptized. And this agrees with the Covenant of Grace in Ezekiel 36:27, where the Lord saith, "I will put my Spirit in them, and cause them to walk in my way, Ezekiel 11:19: "I will give them one heart, and will put my Spirit within them, and will take away the stony heart out of their flesh, and will give them an heart out of their flesh, that they may walk in my statutes, and keep my ordinances to them, and they shall be my people, and I will be their God."

Where you may see, that God is so far from giving his Spirit to the end that souls should plead thereby freedom from the practice of those commanded ordinances of Christ, that on the

---

[54] Acts 9:11.
[55] Acts 9:17–18.

contrary, it is the end why God gives his Spirit to enable and to cause them to walk in his way, and in his ordinances, and in particular, baptism.

And observe, the apostles have left us a bare example only, that they baptize after that Christ powered out the Holy Ghost, and that by the authority received from heaven, but doth command it, as you have heard to all that repent and believe, and to all that receive the Holy Ghost to submit to it.

But again, the baptism of the Holy Ghost and fire, that John foretold of, is clear, was extraordinarily given upon and especial ground and reason fulfilled in Acts 2. The Holy Ghost, falling down in fiery cloven tongues in the sight and view of the bodily eyes, which was that outward sign, and that clear light, and fervent zeal, and love they had, in uttering the wonderful things of God in variety of strange tongues, was the inward thing signified. So that herein the baptism of the Holy Ghost was an outward sign, and an inward thing signified, but there is now no man in the world hath this baptism. Only it is true that the Spirit, in the saving gifts of faith, repentance, and the like, is held to be essential to the obedience of baptism of water, and must be joined together with it, without which it cannot be said to be an ordinance of God, there must be the inward grace as well as the outward sign.

This baptism that the apostle, according to Christ's commission hath left a standing command for, cannot be John's baptism, his holding forth Christ to come, baptizing them in that doctrine. But in this we baptize persons in Christ already come and fully exhibited.

And though it may be objected, that the apostles practiced some things that were abolished, as the circumcising of Timothy and the like. We also say, that as they practiced it among the Jews, so the Apostle Paul to the Gentiles saith, if they be circumcised, Christ should profit them nothing, but they were fal[le]n from grace: and we never find that circumcision was

The Doctrine of Baptism

practiced among the Gentiles that were void of all religion before they taught them.

It is evident in the New Testament that circumcision is abolished as part of the Mosaical Covenant, and yoke of bondage (Gal. 5:1-3), but the case in baptism is clean otherwise.

Whereas you hear the apostle did press Cornelius his family to be baptized, who was a Gentile never acquainted with John's baptism, nor wedded to such a doctrine as that whereby we should think, that Peter did baptize them to condescend to that error or weakness in their minds.

Again, he doth not only simply baptize them, as a liberty that might be done or not done, as you heard before he did in Acts 2. And it cannot be said that the apostles commanded any duty to be done, with a promise of blessing to the right performance of the same, after the Holy Ghost came down upon them, but it must needs be a solemn standing ordinance of God that every soul upon pain of guilt and rebellion against Christ his head and King ought to be subject unto.

But this of baptism hath as aforesaid, many standing laws left in holy record, speaking to all that believe and repent, promising remission of sins, and salvation to the right performance of the same, which proves it to be a standing ordinance of the New Testament.

And truly with the same reason souls may affirm, that Christ ceaseth to be a mediator as to the law of dipping believers ceaseth, so much and no less is affirmed by the soul that saith, the ordinance of baptism is an expired ordinance, he may as well say, Christ is expired and abolished as a fleshly form as some have had confidence to say.

For as in the time of Moses' ministration till there was a change of the priesthood, there could not be a change of the Law no more now, except there be another Christ and Savior come, or another priesthood instead of this Priest and Minister of the New Testament, assure yourselves, there can be no change of his law (as in Heb. 7:12, 18). Therefore such as pretend to profess Christ to be their Savior that came of the seed of David, and the same persons deny and slight this fundamental ordinance of baptism, they do therein testify that they reject Christ in their heart as abolished, and have some pretended fancy—Christ instead of him. It is utterly inconsistent with the faith of the Gospel, and with true religion to hold baptism and the Supper two solemn ordinances and symbols of the New Covenant to be abolished. In Ephesians 4 the apostle, pressing there a visible church union, lays down the main things wherein that union consists, called, saith he, by one hope of their calling, one Spirit, one Lord, one faith, one baptism. This one baptism cannot be meant the Spirit because the Spirit is mentioned distinct, but "baptism" here must needs be meant that standing solemn ordinance of God, commanded to everyone that believes.

Now the apostle, pressing here a church union, doth mention these particulars that are essential to a visible church union, without which they could not walk together, if not in these things agreed, and where a people in all these particulars are one, no other thing coming should make a breach of their union.

Object. But some either souls will object and say, "That believer baptism is an ordinance of God, and he thinks they do well, that are drawn out to practice it, by a power from God. But saith the soul I want a divine power upon my heart, drawing me out to the practice of the same, and that is the let and hinderance in me."

Answ. This objection is grounded upon an error and a mistake, taking for granted, that a man may be a believer, and in a state of grace, and yet void of spiritual power to perform obedience to the commands of God, and that a man that is a Christian may know such a thing to be a command of God, and yet left without ability to perform obedience to the same.

I judge this is a dangerous error and contrary to Scripture. For God doth at the very first conversion, put his law in the heart of his child (as in Heb. 8:10 and as in Ezek. 36:26-27). God is said to put his Spirit in them to that end to cause them to walk in his ways; therefore, in some measure doubtless God doth give his people power to obey him. See in Ezekiel 11:19-20: "I will give them one heart, and I will put a new Spirit within them, and I will take the stony heart out of their flesh, and I will give them an heart of flesh, that they may walk in my statutes, and keep my ordinances, and do them, and they shall be my people, and I will be their God."

Whence you may observe, that God's main drift in making his covenant and giving his Spirit into the hearts of his people, is that they may keep his ordinances, and be able to walk in his ways. Therefore at the first conversion of Paul, God put in him a disposition to obedience; for saith he, "Lord what wouldst thou have me to do?" in Acts 9, and so in Acts 2:37 when they (through the belief of Peter's sermon) were pricked at the heart, they cry out, "Men and brethren, what shall we do?" So you see there was a disposition of heart in their first conversion, to be doing what God should command and teach them to be his will. So we find God gives them power to submit as soon as his will was revealed, for if not so, we should lay an aspersion upon God, that he should enter into a covenant with a soul by way of engagement, and yet neglect to make good his promise, which is, to put his Spirit in him, and to cause him to walk in his ways.

And again further, God gives to every believer, the power of believing, by virtue of which he is enabled to fetch virtue from Christ his head, to strengthen him to duty, and to resist sin; therefore, the apostle thus reasons in the 2 Corinthians 7:1-2: "Dearly beloved, seeing you have these promises, let us cleanse ourselves from all filthiness of flesh and spirit, and perfecting holiness in the fear of God."

Whence observe, the apostle takes for granted the soul having great and precious promises, and faith to draw virtue from them, should thereby oppose sin and perfect holiness in the fear of God. For though it is true, God works to will and do of his good pleasure,[56] yet it is constantly and unfailingly his good pleasure; thus, to work more or less in a soul that is in him thus by faith. And a believer by faith ought to look at himself in a capacity to draw water out of those wells of salvation, for else what differences between a child of God and a wicked man, the form of godliness and the power, if a child of God must be forced to live in a course of disobedience to the solemn worship of God for want of power to obey. And by the same rule we must take for granted that a child of God may be in a state of grace, and want power to resist sin, and upon this ground plead excuse for drunkenness, and covetousness, and theft or uncleanness, and say, though he is a believer, yet he wants power to resist and conquer these sins.

Beloved, thus for any to plead, would be very absurd and contrary to the truth, and the nature of a Christian in a state of grace. And further observe the deceit lying in this objection.

Hath not God given thy soul power to hear the Word of God, and to read, and to meditate, and to pray, and that sometimes earnestly and fervently to God. And is it likely that there wants power to perform obedience to his ordinance of baptism, any more than thou doest perform prayer or other duties which require the same spiritual power, upon due examination? What enabling power is required in the one, more than in the other?

Again consider, thou dost in this, walk by sense, and not by faith (contrary to the apostle [in] 2 Corinthians 5 who saith, "We walk by faith, not by sight"). It is a very childish thing in a Christian to walk by sense only when he feels strength and power sensibly, then he thinks himself able to perform duty, and resist sin; but when he feels not ability and power, then to neglect it. Whereas contrary to this, Christ saith to Paul in the 2 Corinthians 12, "My power shall be made perfect in your

---

[56] Philippians 2:13.

weakness, my grace shall be sufficient for you," and as after, Paul expresseth himself, "When I am weak, then I am strong."

When Paul was made most sensible of his own weakness in himself, then was the time for Paul to be made most strong by faith, in the strength of another. Therefore in Isaiah 45:24: "In thee Lord have I righteousness and strength. In him shall they boast." And the Psalmist saith in Psalm 73:4: "Though my heart fail and flesh fail, yet God will never fail, he is the strength of my life, and my portion forever." So that when a man's own sense, his heart fails, his flesh fails, then is the only time for God's strength to appear in weakness. This is the way of living by faith, and the way which God's believing children have been carried. Therefore, we find Jonah, when (in his own sense) he was cast out of God's sight, then he resolved to look towards God's holy temple, and cried to God out of the belly of hell, as in Jonah 2; therefore, surely this objection hath no weight in it.

Object. But some other soul say, "I grant the practice of baptism to be an ordinance of God, and the way of such churches that walk under the baptism of believers to be that only justifiable practice in the Gospel, and could willingly walk with them and be baptized were it not for their rigidness in that they will have no communion with any (though godly) that are not baptized."

Answ. To this I answer by way of distinction between church union and communion, and personal union and communion. Now if we find a soul not baptized, nor joined to any church, and happily ignorant of baptism, yet if I ground in my own heart, to judge that soul to be godly, and not an enemy to the truth, and Gospel of Christ but a soul willing to hear and learn what truth God shall further reveal unto him, and so having ground to judge such a soul to have union and personal communion with the Lord, in such a case I ought to imitate the Lord in owning a communion with such a Christian, in like manner, as for example.

Cornelius and his family, having a personal union with the Lord and communion with him, before Peter preached to him, and he not being an obstinate, professed enemy against the Law of Christ, but contrarywise saying to Peter, "We are here to hear whatsoever is commanded thee of God."

Therefore the Spirit of God falling down upon them, they spake with new tongues, and glorified God, and Peter and the six baptized brethren bring with them, no question did join in Spirit and heart, in that present spiritual service, which Cornelius and his family did perform to God, they none of them at that interim of time, being baptized nor convinced that baptism was an ordinance of God. For till Peter had consulted with the brethren, he did not press baptism upon them. And therefore we find that he did instruct them, after consultation which he had with the brethren, saying, "How should we forbid water that these should not be baptized, that have received the Holy Ghost as well as we."

And Paul in like manner, between the time of Christ had converted him, and his coming to Ananias saith, that Paul was "a chosen vessel, for behold he now prayeth," manifesting that he owned Paul in that service.

Now he, being in a teachable, godly frame (though ignorant of baptism), in prayer God had communion with him. In like manner I judge from these Scripture examples [that] it is lawful for a baptized person to have fellowship in prayer or speaking with any such soul which he is persuaded of to be godly, and that is not a professed enemy to any command of God.

But God hath not, as we find, ever had any church union or communion with any soul that was unbaptized. It is clear that the ordinance of the Supper is committed to a church, yea to a ministerial assembly gathered according to Christ's commission (Matt. 28:19-20). Where I understand the order there binding is this: First, the ministers should teach the nations, or make them disciples by teaching. Second, the command is

The Doctrine of Baptism

baptizing them. What then? Such are that are made disciples by teaching. Third, the command is to teach them to observe whatsoever Christ hath commanded. What then is here meant but such as are disciples and baptized, "teaching to observe whatsoever I commanded you?" "And I will be with you to the end of the world," that is, he will be with a people, first converted, secondly baptized, thirdly walking in the practical observation of all other administrations of God's house as these eleven did, and those they converted. I say this his promise is to be with this people to the end of the world.

And this order is binding, that as a minister is commanded to baptize one made a disciple, and not any other, so he is commanded to put them upon the practical observation of all his laws, and they only, and till they are baptized, they are not, nor cannot be admitted into a visible church to partake of the Supper of the Lord.

And that this is the true meaning of Christ in the commission appears by his apostles' ministry and practice, who by the infallible gifts of the Holy Ghost, were guided unfailingly thus to preach and practice, as in Acts 2:37-38 with verses 41 and 42. First he teacheth them the doctrine of Jesus Christ, they hearing that were pricked at the heart, and inquiring of Peter, and the rest of the apostles, what they should do, he saith, "Repent and be baptized every one of you." See how he presseth the same order here as Christ doth in the commission, and afterwards in the 41st verse, it is said, "So many as gladly received the Word of God were baptized, and the same day there was added to the Church about three thousand souls," by faith and baptism, "and they continued in the apostles' doctrine and fellowship, in breaking of bread and prayer."

Therefore the way that Christ hath ordained is, that souls should be joined or added to the Church by faith and baptism according to that word in 1 Corinthians 12:13: "We are all baptized by one Spirit into one body."

Now though the Spirit (as the inward thing signified) be here spoken of, yet the outward sign is also included, as might be by other scriptures cleared. Thus Cornelius his family were converted, then baptized before they were constituted in a church.

So the gaoler's, and Lydia's, and the church of Samaria in Acts 8 were all gathered by faith and dipping. And for a minister to gather a church any other way is to go not only in an untrodden path, but cross and point-blank contrary to the doctrine and practice of the apostles, and thereby slighting the rules of Christ in the commission by which the apostles' doctrine and practice was guided, and which all the ministers of the Gospel ought to be guided by.

9
Why the Ordinance of Baptism is Administered but Once, the Ordinance of the Lord's Supper Often

But yet further, the ordinance of baptism is to confirm our regeneration, new birth, and union with Christ in his death, burial, and resurrection (Rom. 6:3-5 with Col. 2:12; Titus 3:5), and therefore is to be received but once, as a man is to be regenerated but once, born but once, and changed from death to life but once. But that ordinance of God, viz. the Supper is for Christians' growth, and increase of grace and of constant use, to show forth Christ's death till he come, and therefore to be received often.

Now it must needs be a profanation of this ordinance of God in them, and that is, to admit persons to that ordinance, which principally for Christian growth before you have admitted them to that ordinance which is for planting them into Christ, signifying the confirmation or waiting of regeneration, and the new birth and union with Christ, the true stock and root from whence all spiritual growth is to be expected.

Therefore, baptism must be the first ordinance dispensed or administered after conversion, before the Supper. So that it would be a profanation of the ordinances of God to divert their proper order, end and use, to which our holy and jealous God hath appointed them. It is a tender point for those that profess themselves friends to Christ, the bridegroom, to be venturing to take his peculiar privilege or prerogative, out of his hands as to order and dispose of his own order in his solemn worship, contrary to his commission.

I do judge such a man that hath not a tender conscience in such cases, is in that much unlike Christ, and shows much carnality because as you have heard, God will have the honor to direct his people, both for the matter and manner of their worship, and order of his house.

What things are essential to a particular visible Church
But again as you have heard before (in Eph. 4:3-4), there is by the apostle mentioned these things that are essential to a particular visible church union which are these:

First, to be all called into one hope of our calling, which the poor children, which some admit into their society by sprinkling, are not called to the same hope that believers are called into.

Again, "One body, one Spirit, one faith, one Lord, and one baptism, one God and Father of us all."

Now it is impossible that a people should together acceptably, that have not hope of one and the same glorious inheritance, that have not one and the same Spirit and assistance and guidance in his holy worship, and that have not one and the same faith, but in the doctrine of faith do mainly differ one from another. And it is an essential difference, inconsistent with communion, that the members of one church should own two baptisms, the sprinkling of infants and dipping believers, and this ordinance of baptism is one of the essentials of a true visible church.

And lastly, they are to own "one God and Father of all." Here you have from this text a ground why such as are not enlightened in the Lord's baptism cannot be admitted into church fellowship, because in one and the same fellowship, there is to be owned as "one hope, one Spirit, one Lord, one faith," so one and the same baptism.

Again the main end of Church fellowship, is, that they there do practice whatsoever Christ had commanded as you have heard before in Matt. 28:20 and as Cornelius saith in Acts 10: "We are here to hear whatsoever is commanded thee of God,"

The Doctrine of Baptism

and saith Christ, "Ye are my friends if you do whatsoever I commanded you."

And this is without doubt, that the true and lawful ministry in Christ's Church is to see that all the members practice the observation of whatsoever he hath commanded; and so to see all the laws of Christ put in execution. For that cause hath Christ given into his Church, not only the key of doctrine, but also the key of discipline, that if any soul in a church shall be known, wittingly or willingly, to neglect any duty that the Lord hath commanded by his holy Word, especially a fundamental ordinance of the New Testament, as is baptism and the Supper of the Lord. It is without all question, that such a soul, standing out in that disobedience, ought to be cast out of the church speedily for the same, without which the Church allowing or conniving at, or tolerating a soul in one course of known disobedience, do thereby make the sin their own, the whole people becoming really guilty of his sin and impiety. And as the apostle saith, "Thus will the whole lump be leavened,"[57] and that church unchurched.

Amongst men he that concealeth murder, and is privy and consenting to it, and will agree to tolerate it, is reckoned a murderer; in like manner in the case of theft. Now the main end of church fellowship and ministerial power is to destroy sin, and execute the power of Christ against it, and not to be the fosterers and countenancers of sin, which you are if you agree to admit any person into your fellowship that refuseth to submit to baptism, that plain, solemn ordinance of the New Testament, let his pretence be what it will be. That person that is not brought over to yield obedience to whatsoever Christ hath commanded, is not (while so disobedient) fit matter for a visible gospel church, especially in those his fundamental ordinances as prayer, hearing, baptism, and the Supper of the Lord, thanksgiving, contribution to the necessity of the saints, and

---

[57] 1 Corinthians 5:6.

maintenance of an official ministry according to the ability that God gives them. By the same rule, and upon the same ground that you will tolerate some members in the church to live in the neglect of baptism, you must tolerate such as neglect to hear the word, and others that will not, according to ability, contribute to pious, charitable uses, and others that will not pray in half a year or a twelve month, under the pretense they are not moved to that duty, and others that will in gross manner neglect the duty of particular callings or relations, which the apostle in 2 Thessalonians doth give rule to be withdrawn from, which is as the rest. But the neglect of duty, nay this practice lays a foundation for all disobedience, and for gathering an assembly of rebels, let me alone in my sin, and I will let thee alone in thine.

But may some say, is a godly man's omitting to be baptized or dipped a sin? Yes, certainly it is, for [in] 1 John 3:6, the apostle saith, sin is a transgression of the Law.

Now you have heard several laws of the New Testament do command that such as believe and repent should be baptized; therefore, to neglect is a transgression of those laws; and sincere obedience is universal obedience, by this saith David, "I know I shall not be ashamed when I have respect to all thy commandments."

Unbaptized persons not to be admitted into Church fellowship
But further consider, if you receive a person into communion that doth not submit to the Lord's baptism, that soul justifies still a corrupt baptism that he had in his infancy, and consequently is not ashamed of all he hath done amiss, which Ezekiel speaks of, but still stands in fellowship and communion with a church and ministry which, by the bishops' power dispensed the same, and you, receiving such a soul into communion, receive that church and ministry, from which he had his supposed baptism, and must certainly own all those churches which that ministry stood in fellowship with, that so baptized him.

THE DOCTRINE OF BAPTISM

Therefore, it is a sad and serious matter who it is that is admitted into fellowship in the true Church of Christ, and I would admonish souls to be careful that they do what they do in good order. God, it is said, made a breach upon Uzziah because he did not do what he did in due order.

Object. But some may say, "Faith in Christ brings a soul into sonship, and so to a right in all the privileges in God's house."

Answ. It is true, faith and repentance doth entitle a soul, but repentance according to the Gospel is a change of the heart, and a resolution to obey God in all his commandments. Such a repentance only the Church of Christ ought to own in those members they receive. And therefore thought they ought to receive the weak in faith, yet they have no rule to receive them but by faith and baptism. So that though faith gives an interest to baptism, yet faith and baptism, are to prepare and fit a soul for communion. "So many as gladly received the word were baptized, and the same day there were added to the Church about three thousand souls, and they continued in the apostles' doctrine, and fellowship, in breaking of bread and prayer."

So here you see the Word of Christ our Lord (unto whom we ought to submit) that those only who were baptized were admitted into the fellowship of the saints and to breaking of bread, and therefore we upon these grounds may not admit any member in communion into the church of Christ but by baptism.

But some may object and say, "There are many godly souls that do think they are baptized already in their infancy. And till they be convinced of that error, cannot you have church communion with them?"

To this I answer, I dare not say, but precious souls to God in these times as well as formerly, may be (in that point) in darkness; I do not censure the case of such. But sure I am, that if they judge their own baptism or sprinkling in their infancy to be an ordinance of God, they cannot but judge it a duty still to practice the same upon their own infants, being faithful to their principle. Then, how can a church and true ministry that judges dipping of believers a duty, and the other to be a grievous and provoking sin, admit such a person into communion that resolves to live not only in the neglect of a solemn duty, but in a great and heinous sin in the judgment of that church and ministry that is to admit him which the justifying of his baptism must needs be?

Wherefore hath Christ set up in his Gospel Church his ordinance of excommunication, or casting forth out of the church, if [those] persons may be admitted that are resolved to live in both a sin of omission and commission, and such as have not repented of that sin of sprinkling children?

So then, that person that lives impenitently in any one known sin (known I mean to the church), if that church have communion with that person in that sin, the sin becomes the church's sin.

Object. "But he liveth in this sin through ignorance."

Answ. That we presuppose or else the Scripture would send us little hopes of charity, as to this good estate. For to know a sin to be a sin, and to live in it, doubtless it cannot stand with grace; therefore, it is generally concluded that the contempt of any ordinance of God is damnable, but not the simple neglect of it, being upon scruples or doubts of conscience unanswered; but the church knows it be a sin, and therefore they are not to have communion with it.

Object. But some say, "I am afraid some persons do rest in ordinances, and place that in them which is due to Christ only, which is some offence to me, and hath kept me off from that practice."

Answ. There is no sound ground for this objection, from either our profession or practice, for we do profess salvation, justification, and spiritual welfare to be merely of the grace of God in Christ, and that by faith only. Our obedience to Christ ought to be performed from a principle of regeneration and union with

Christ by faith, and answerable is our practice in that we dare not put any soul on obedience but from the root. For before we baptize any soul, we prove whether a true work of conversion be wrought in his heart or no; and whether he have union with Christ, and dare not admit children because that we judge that they have not a principle of Christ in them from whence they should submit to baptism.

And further, let me say, then, it is easy for a soul to forebear resting in duties that doth not perform them. But that which is worthy in a Christian is to walk as strictly in obedience to all the commands of God, as though he would be saved by his obedience, and to rest as fully upon Christ and his blood, and the love of God therein revealed as if he had done nothing at all, accounting himself an unprofitable servant. And whereas you say you fear they rest in duties, that fear and jealousy in you (I fear) is your sin, and possibly many flow from that inbred enmity and prejudice that is apt to be in every man's heart against the pure ways of God. Or else it proceeds from the malice of the devil, suggesting such thoughts into thy heart. For thou enterest into the hearts of such people, and judgest their very intents in this thy fear and jealousy, and therefore beware of this snare.

But further, suppose some souls should be so far left of God that walk in the practice of the ordinances as to rest in them, is that a ground of thee to excuse thee, to live in sinful neglect of them? In a word, there can be no objection come into thy heart, tending to hinder thee from this duty, and to keep thee from thy obedience to thy Lord and King, but it must needs be from the flesh or from the devil, and therefore beware of them. Suppose thy judgment inclined to such a latitude as that thou couldst have communion with unbaptized persons, consider with a tender conscience what hath been said, and I hope it may much satisfy thee in that objection. But I suppose thou didst not be satisfied with what hath been said, but still judge that thy liberty thou canst not but say it's clear in the New Testament, and out of doubt, that such believing and being baptized ought to have church fellowship together with the practice of ordinances? Is that a justifiable argument to keep thee off from communion with such as (out of doubt) thou mayest, according to rule, have communion with and further that thou canst not but say, is thy duty to have communion with?

10
Conclusion:
The Commands of Christ Must Not Be Disputed

Therefore I would in all tenderness admonish and warn all that fear God, to be more conformable and observe the rules of Christ, and not to harbor such gross error in thy mind, as to think thou mayest at thy pleasure dispute the commands and ordinances of Christ.

The Apostle Paul in Galatians 1:16 saith, "He conferred not with flesh and blood, but he presently obeyed the heavenly voice." And Christ when God by his Spirit directed him to go to the doctors in the temple, to hear them, and ask them questions, he without so much as acquainting his father or mother, obeyed the Lord, though to their great grief and trouble in going. And then in Philippians 2:14 our obedience should be without murmuring, repining or any more ado. And, in Luke 5:5, Peter had been fishing all night and caught nothing, therefore had little hopes to catch any fish, yet saith he, "At thy word I will cast down my net;" he did not dispute the commands of Christ, though his own experience and skill did utterly testify against what Christ had commanded, as to sense, that there could be no good effect produced, yet at thy word, saith he, I will cast in my net. As David in Psalm 119 [says], "I made haste to keep thy righteous precepts," for delaying of obedience doth harden the heart, and give place to the tempter. Therefore I would advise all godly souls to drink in this as a maxim, that if you find an express law of Christ given to a believer, that it is utterly unlawful to dispute or to question the practice of it upon any pretense whatsoever, or to admit any objection against it. For amongst men both in civil and military authority, they will not have their laws disputed, who may err greatly in making those laws. But our righteous God (whose laws be sure are just) will not have his disputed, and therefore, as before, when Christ bid Peter [to] cast down his net into the sea, saith he, "I have been all night and catched nothing, yet notwithstanding, at thy word I will cast down my net." Where, observe, though what Christ commanded him, his skill, experience, and reason might have strongly objected against, yet he learned this, that there could not be any justifiable ground to bear him out in disputing Christ's laws.

And thus you have an example in Abraham in sacrificing Isaac, who was the promised seed, "And when God called him, he followed God, not knowing whether he went." And Noah, when he built an ark for the saving of his house; and Jacob upon the command of God, carrying away his family three days journey before Laban, and the family knew of it. There might have been much dispute against these things, but these holy men of God had learned not to give place to the pride and rebellion of their unmortified reason and understanding, which many souls, for want of more grace and soundness of judgment, give way to, in our days. But they did obey the word of God's command without any more a do, as the apostle's rule is, Philippians 2:12-15: "Wherefore my beloved, as you have always obeyed, not as in my presence only, but now much more in my absence, work out your own salvation with fear and trembling, for it is God that worketh in you to will and to do of his own good pleasure; Do all things without murmurings and disputings, that you may be blameless and harmless, the sons of God without rebuke in the midst of a crooked and perverse nation, amongst whom you shine as lights in the world."

Scripture Index

Old Testament

Genesis
- 3:15 63
- 3:16 63
- 4:4 .... 107, 110
- 6:5 .... 99, 110
- 9:4 99
- 9:26 100
- 11:7 101
- 11:17 101
- 12:3 .... 64, 73, 103, 108
- 12:4 72
- 15:5 65
- 15:5-6 .... 75, 108
- 17:13 .... 69, 128
- 17:14 85
- 17:17 .... 54, 89
- 17:10-11 87
- 17:12-13 82
- 17:7-8 70
- 18:18 .... 103, 107
- 21:2 101
- 22:18 .... 66, 73, 122
- 25:1 101
- 25:23 102
- 25:26 101

Exodus
- 13:12-13 99
- 34:19 99
- 40:15 70

Leviticus
- 17:10-11 99

Numbers
- 25:13 69

Deuteronomy
- 4:2 148
- 7:2 117

7:7 102
- 7:12-13 81
- 7:2-3 99
- 18:4 99
- 30:15 81
- 30:12-14 130

2 Samuel
- 23:5 61

2 Kings
- 5:14 37

2 Chronicles
- 26:14-15 146
- 26:19-21 147

Nehemiah
- 10:29 59

Job
- 8:8 83
- 8:10 83
- 11:11 111
- 15:10 83
- 20:23 111

Psalms
- 97:10 63

Proverbs
- 3:19 99
- 8:9 111
- 23:23 24

Isaiah
- 8:28 84
- 9:6 41
- 10:22-23 91
- 28:16 41
- 42:6 63
- 43:2 40
- 45:24 156
- 50:1 86

65:23 123
Jeremiah
  2:23–24 111
  7:31 145
  8:9 145
  11:2–5 72
  17:9 20
  33:15 85
Ezekiel
  11:19–20 154

14:4 149
18:9–10 95
36:27 151
36:25–27 59
Joel
  2:28–32 150
Micah
  7:1 99
Habakkuk
  2:4 134

New Testament

Matthew
- 3:17 ... 107
- 11:25 ... 22
- 16:23-24 ... 24
- 19:13 ... 135
- 28:19 ... 45
- 28:19-20 ... 149

Mark
- 1:8 ... 37, 38
- 1:16 ... 37
- 7:7 ... 144
- 10:13 ... 135
- 10:13-15 ... 137
- 16:16 ... 40
- 26:26 ... 43

Luke
- 1:35 ... 142
- 3:2-3 ... 38
- 5:5 ... 169
- 12:50 ... 40
- 19:38 ... 22
- 19:39 ... 22
- 19:40 ... 22

John
- 1:23 ... 38
- 3:8 ... 38
- 3:16 ... 41
- 3:17 ... 41
- 3:18 ... 109
- 3:4-5 ... 92
- 4:2 ... 135
- 4:22 ... 101
- 4:23 ... 96
- 5:28-29 ... 107
- 6:27 ... 41
- 6:69 ... 108
- 6:32-33 ... 129
- 7:22 ... 127
- 8:24 ... 92, 109, 114
- 8:31 ... 93
- 14:6 ... 108
- 15:15 ... 23
- 16:8 ... 42

Acts
- 2:37 ... 30, 42, 154, 158
- 2:38 ... 45, 149
- 2:39 ... 113
- 2:37-38 ... 30
- 2:40-42 ... 45
- 2:41-42 ... 97
- 3:26 ... 64
- 4:12 ... 92, 108
- 5:31 ... 62
- 8:20 ... 82
- 8:32 ... 46
- 8:33 ... 40
- 8:35-36 ... 40
- 8:38 ... 131, 148
- 8:12-13 ... 46
- 8:38-39 ... 38
- 9:11 ... 150
- 9:15 ... 41
- 9:17-18 ... 150
- 10:48 ... 45, 144
- 11:18 ... 62
- 13:45-46 ... 115, 142
- 15:1 ... 127
- 15:9 ... 109
- 15:10 ... 128
- 15:1-33 ... 22
- 15:14-15 ... 47
- 18:8 ... 48
- 18:27 ... 62
- 19:9 ... 115
- 22:16 ... 45, 150

Romans
- 1:17 ... 134
- 2:25 ... 71
- 3:9 ... 90, 108
- 4:1 ... 128
- 4:3 ... 65
- 4:11 ... 76

4:12 66
4:14 109
4:16 109
4:25 42
4:1–2 .... 65, 73
4:14–17 78
4:17–18 65
6:4................................39
6:6................................39
6:8................................ 40
6:11.............................. 40
6:3–5 161
6:4–5 40
8:30............................ 113
9:5................................ 42
9:8................................ 66
9:13 42
9:31 91
9:27–28.......................91
9:7–8 110
11:5..............................91
11:17 81
1 Corinthians
1:2 96
2:9–10 42
5:6............................... 163
7:14 ....115, 116
10:2 .... 38, 126
10:6 129
10:1–3........................126
11:6.............................. 48
11:25 107
11:28 131
12:13 158
15:21 107
15:29...........................39
2 Corinthians
1:20 .... 63, 86
5:16 125
5:17..............................125
7:1–2...........................155
Galatians
1:16 169
3:2...............................127

3:3 79
3:8.....................108, 122
3:16 66
3:17..................... 86, 107
3:19 126
3:27 39
3:29 66
3:28–29......................109
4:4 41
4:21 140
5:6 122
5:1–3...71, 72, 128, 141, 152
6:15 125
6:12–13 71
Ephesians
1:3 107
1:6 107
4:24............................. 117
4:10–12 42
4:3–4 162
Philippians
1:28 62
2:13 155
2:14 169
2:12–15 170
Colossians
2:8 148
2:12 ....39, 161
2 Timothy
2:25 62
Hebrews
2:14 42
2:25 42
6:12 108
7:12 153
7:18 153
8:6...............................80
8:10 154
8:13 121
8:6–7 125
9:9 82
9:15 114
9:15–16 58
10:12........................... 42